T0351011

The Shortest Hour

Independent directors of corporate boards understand the importance of cyber security as a business issue. Increased regulatory requirements, the onslaught of breaches, as well as the replacement of the corporate network perimeter with more third-party partnerships have all contributed to cyber security rising to the top of enterprise risks. Yet, many directors only receive a few brief cyber security updates during the year. Moreover, many directors have devoted their careers to other important business disciplines and may not fully grasp the technical concepts of cyber security.

The challenge is that many publications on board cyber security governance address the topic at such a high level that it removes the important context of the cyber security details—or covers the topic too deeply with hard-to-understand technical language. These resources may often provide lists of security questions for directors to ask of their management team, but they do not provide the answers to the questions so that actionable oversight can be performed. What I would have wanted, and why you are probably reading this book summary, is a resource that delivers the questions to ask but also provides the answers and in a narrative, easy-to-understand style.

An award-winning Chief Information Security Officer with over two decades of working with multiple Fortune 500 boards, Lee Parrish provides an example-laden vision to improve cyber security governance in the boardroom. Additionally, Lee deciphers the technical jargon to increase the reader's cyber fluency—not to make you a cyber expert but to help you be able to ask direct questions, understand the answers provided, challenge strategies, and advise on important cyber decisions.

Pick up your copy of *The Shortest Hour: An Applied Approach to Boardroom Governance of Cyber Security* today and start your journey on achieving more effective cyber security oversight.

Want to learn more? Please visit www.novelsecurity.com

Security, Audit and Leadership Series

Series Editor: Dan Swanson, Dan Swanson and Associates, Ltd., Winnipeg, Manitoba, Canada.

The *Security, Audit and Leadership Series* publishes leading-edge books on critical subjects facing security and audit executives as well as business leaders. Key topics addressed include Leadership, Cybersecurity, Security Leadership, Privacy, Strategic Risk Management, Auditing IT, Audit Management and Leadership

Rising from the Mailroom to the Boardroom
Unique Insights for Governance, Risk, Compliance and Audit Leaders
Bruce Turner

Operational Auditing
Principles and Techniques for a Changing World (Second Edition)
Hernan Murdock

CyRM™
Mastering the Management of Cybersecurity
David X Martin

Why CISOs Fail (Second Edition)
Barak Engel

Riding the Wave
Applying Project Management Science in the Field of Emergency Management
Andrew Boyarsky

The Shortest Hour
An Applied Approach to Boardroom Governance of Cyber Security
Lee Parrish

For more information about this series, please visit: https://www.routledge.com/Internal-Audit-and-IT-Audit/book-series/CRCINTAUDITA

The Shortest Hour

An Applied Approach to Boardroom Governance of Cyber Security

Lee Parrish

CRC Press
Taylor & Francis Group
Boca Raton London New York

CRC Press is an imprint of the
Taylor & Francis Group, an **informa** business

Designed cover image: © Shutterstock

First edition published 2025
by CRC Press
2385 NW Executive Center Drive, Suite 320, Boca Raton FL 33431

and by CRC Press
4 Park Square, Milton Park, Abingdon, Oxon, OX14 4RN

CRC Press is an imprint of Taylor & Francis Group, LLC

© 2025 Lee Parrish

ISBN: 9781032757940 (hbk)
ISBN: 9781032761633 (pbk)
ISBN: 9781003477341 (ebk)

DOI: 10.1201/9781003477341

Typeset in Sabon
by Newgen Publishing UK

For Nancy: To the moon and back again...

Contents

About the Author

Lee Parrish is an award-winning technology executive with over two decades of unique experience in blending cyber security expertise with essential business competencies. As a chief information security officer, he has built customized cyber security strategies for global Fortune 500 corporations and has led real-world incident responses to cyber events. Lee has served as a trusted advisor on cyber security to multiple boards consisting of chief executive officers, a former White House chief of staff, retired high-ranking military officers, and a former U.S. Presidential candidate.

Lee possesses two graduate degrees and is certified as both a Boardroom Qualified Technology Expert and a Certified Information Systems Security Professional. He has published numerous articles in industry journals, contributed to a best-selling information security book, and authored a children's book on cyber security. He is a frequent speaker at international security conferences and a guest on various podcasts.

Lee is a combat veteran of the United States Marine Corps.

Preface

I believe we are the sum of all the people and experiences that came before us, each providing inputs to our lives that collectively make up who we are, sprinkled with a little of our own individuality. A book is a lot like this too, I think. I am merely a storyteller of the collection of inputs that have affected my life and contributed to the content of this book. Whether it was two decades of collaborating with incredible teammates in large corporations, partnering with the highest levels of corporate governance, or an impactful two-minute conversation with an interesting stranger in an airport, each interaction has helped shape my thoughts on so many different topics. For our purposes here, my thoughts are focused on the management and oversight of a cyber security program for a corporation.

This book is not a technical guide; that is an important theme of this book: cyber security is not a technical issue. It is a business issue that deserves significant attention from business executives. Of course, technology plays a crucial role in cyber security but only as a tool, a partial means to a larger end. It is very much like an adversary who uses malicious software (malware) as a mechanism to achieve something that is deeper than the technology, something that is at the heart of the issue: their malevolent intent combined with their criminal behavior. As you will read in the following chapters, I believe there should be a shift in how cyber security should evolve in the boardroom. I hope that this book inspires change and imagines a vision for where information security oversight could evolve.

Lee Parrish
December 2023

For feedback and inquiries regarding this book and/or speaking engagement requests, please contact the author by visiting: www.novelsecurity.com

Introduction

Business is a dynamic discipline, constantly evolving, requiring corporate directors to advise on a variety of topics that aim to positively impact top-line revenue growth and improve bottom-line efficiencies, as well as pay notice to regulatory and legal matters for the company. Each director is heavily involved in multiple initiatives that extend from short-term actions to long-term growth. Each year, new disciplines and regulatory requirements are introduced that require attention as well, without removing the traditional categories from the director's suite of responsibilities.

When special events take place, such as bankruptcy, mergers, acquisitions, and divestitures, it is realistic that the director's attention shifts to those events but without losing sight of the other baseline responsibilities. All of this is done as guardians of shareholder value. It is not a passive role and requires significant consideration to a variety of domains.

This book reinforces a discipline that will require a director's attention at even greater levels than ever before: *cyber security*. My goal in writing this book is not to make the reader an expert in cyber security. Instead, it is to provide valuable tips and information so that the Director can ask the proper questions of their corporate leadership team *and* understand the answers provided to them to ensure that their cyber security program is optimal and ready to react to business disruption. This book is for you, the newly appointed director, or a seasoned board member being introduced to the emerging boardroom topic of cyber security.

This book can also be a valuable resource for C-level executives who want to understand more about cyber security but in an easy-to-understand format. As directors become even more educated on the discipline of cyber security, your cyber knowledge will be needed to answer their questions and importantly make informed decisions. Your chief information security officer (CISO) can help fill in the details of what you learn from these pages and then help you to apply them to your organization.

Lastly, my colleagues in the cyber security industry may leverage this book for various reasons. Perhaps for someone wanting to pursue a CISO role, my hope is the insights I've gained from over two decades of working with boards will provide you with what to expect from the role. For my seasoned peers, you are no doubt familiar with the concepts you are about to read, but hopefully there will be a few tips that are new and can be added to your security program.

As we collectively explore new ways to enhance cyber security within the corporate governance structure, several industry publications, books, and social media posts have surfaced that provide very good discussion points on this topic. Many of these effectively highlight the need for cyber security to be discussed more frequently at the board level, increasing cyber fluency among board members, and the impacts for improving (or not improving) the dialogue within the boardroom. Additionally, I have seen published guidance with a roster of questions that directors can ask of their CISO pertaining to cyber security within their company. What I wanted, and probably why you are reading these pages too, is a source of information that not only provides questions that address common concerns in cyber but also provides a very general understanding of the topics so that you can understand the answers provided to you in order to deliver informed business guidance.

In some areas, it may feel that I am covering areas a bit more deeply, but the broad underpinnings are important so that you may understand the answers to your questions. My commitment to you is that I'll only detail enough for you to grasp the concepts and nothing further. Your CISO can go more deeply into the subject, should you desire. If the reader has not heard it previously, it is important to note here that when it comes to cyber breaches, it is not a question of "if it will happen" but "when it will happen". Never has the importance of cyber security context, understanding a topic and the impacts to your company, been so critical.

As those of you who work on more than one board can attest, not all information security programs are the same. Based on the unique risks to the company, their corporate strategies, operational model, financial position, and a host of other characteristics, it is natural (and necessary) for each company to have a customized security program that works for them but may not work for other companies. Despite what some consultancies may boast, there is no single strategy, no one size fits all type of security model that can be applied across multiple corporations. Each security strategy is as unique as a fingerprint, but the underpinnings and foundations of the strategy are as common as a finger. There are not too many instances where there may be an absolute correct way or an absolute wrong way to address a cyber security issue. More often than not, there are many nuanced considerations that require deeper analysis of the issues. My goal is to help the reader identify the core foundations while giving ideas on what to look for in each unique strategy.

In my twenty-three-year career as an information security executive, I have had the unique privilege of working with several diverse and exceptional boards across multiple industries: aerospace/defense, financial services, technology, manufacturing, retail, consumer products, engineering, and data marketing. With the exception of one, all the boards I've worked with had international responsibilities across hundreds of countries; and one board in particular had a non-U.S.-based governance structure. Each board, much like each company, has a personality: a unique blend of executives and challenges that differentiates itself from others.

I have been fortunate insofar as the levels of interactions I experienced with each board were extremely varied. Of course, there is the traditional CISO engagement with a committee, usually the audit committee (more on this later), where most CISOs interact. Additionally, I often briefed the full board on matters of strategic security planning or in the wake of a significant incident response. When a new director was onboarded, I provided a one-on-one briefing on the state of information security for the corporation in which they were about to embark. Moreover, there were times when I met with directors or committee chairpersons to conduct special projects on their behalf. All of these interactions gave me first-hand knowledge of what was top of mind for each of them, as well as a view into where opportunities to enhance corporate governance on matters of cyber security reside.

The members of the boards I worked with were equally diverse, all from various backgrounds with a unique contribution to the overall team. Whether it was a United States Presidential candidate, a White House chief of staff, retired high-ranking members of the military, or chief executive officers of Fortune 500 corporations, each director provided a distinctive opportunity for me to grow my competencies in working with boards. If not for each of them and the opportunities they provided me, this book would not be possible.

Section One

Enhancing Board Oversight

Chapter 1

The threat landscape

Cyber threats to organizations, as well as the malicious actors that exploit them, constantly evolve. So much so that by the time that you finish this book, material shifts in cyber threats may have already taken place, or at the very least, more than a few corporations will have been breached. Yet, there are some foundational threats that remain consistent, threatening our corporate infrastructures; and these are the threats that I will highlight in this chapter. In doing so, it provides a good foundation for what any organization connected to the Internet faces on a daily basis. Moreover, it is well known that all of us have varying levels of understanding of cyber security, so starting with the foundational concepts helps to explain what the information security industry is trying to achieve in their daily work, for readers of all skill levels.

WE ARE ALL TARGETS

During my career as an information security executive, I have heard many senior executives tell me that their organization isn't in the type of industry or a company that would be a target for adversaries. "We are just a small company, not a large aerospace and defense corporation; why would anyone want to target us?"

While this may have historically been true, in recent years the adversaries have added new capabilities to their attack models so that sensitive data isn't the only thing they seek to exploit. Data has value, but that value has a shelf life that may often diminish over time. Historically, criminals would steal data to sell on the dark web[1] for monetary gain. But as the data sits on the darkest corners of the Internet, consumers change credit card numbers or do other actions that make the data obsolete over time. Our adversaries realized this, and while stealing data is still very much prevalent in our industry, especially for trade secrets, personally identifiable information, access credentials, and other sensitive corporate data, they added ransomware to their arsenal of cyber weaponry.

DOI: 10.1201/9781003477341-3

Ransomware leveled the playing field for all industries as it relates to becoming a target. It doesn't matter what industry a company is in; threat actors will seek to attack most anyone leveraging this tactic. Malicious software called ransomware encrypts a system so that it is unusable without the decryption keys, which the attacker possesses. For a fee (ransom), the threat actor promises to deliver the keys so that the system can be used again. If the victim does not pay, the system remains locked, and the adversary may threaten to post their data publicly. Leveraging this technique means the attacker (if paid) realizes one hundred percent of the economic value of the attack, each and every time they attack; there is no dilution of the value that may be seen in stealing data and selling it on the dark web.

In recent years, we've seen a nuance to ransomware that exploits the victim company as detailed previously but adds a malicious twist insofar as if a ransom is indeed paid to unlock the system, the attacker then threatens to post the data publicly if *another* ransom (double ransom technique) is not paid. The decision to pay or not pay a ransom is a significant debate across corporate boardrooms and is a topic I'll cover in more detail later in this book.

Malicious actors are often motivated by financial gain, which makes disruption to industries and companies such as power plants, lifesaving healthcare, financial services, or mass transit attractive to them – in hopes of large payouts to keep critical services operational. Simultaneously, these are the industries that often may employ more robust cyber security programs than other companies; not impenetrable but potentially more difficult to bypass. Attacking small- to mid-cap companies, which may not possess as vigorous of a security program as critical infrastructures, can still be just as profitable for the attacker. At the same time, all victim companies, no matter the size or industry, feel similar impacts to their manufacturing, product development, and service delivery capabilities as a result of a breach.

As adversaries continue to evolve, it has widened their attack surface beyond certain industries historically deemed critical. All companies, organizations, or any entity that conducts business online is a viable target.

THE PERIMETER IS DEAD

Traditionally, corporations leveraged networks that had a perimeter, with security controls layered around it, with the notion that malicious and unauthorized persons were on the outside of that boundary and trusted employees were on the inside of the perimeter. Such an environment provided some advantages to security but did not produce absolute protection. It was realistic for two companies or programs to contractually require the installation of a firewall between the two zones but if that firewall was configured to allow network traffic to freely flow in and out without filtering, proper security was not provided, but the spirit of the contract was met. Nevertheless, securing a defined area was indeed advantageous, albeit not realistic today given the technological improvements and cost reduction opportunities available in the market.

Through the advent of digital initiatives, Internet-connected manufacturing, increased third-party partnerships, cloud computing, artificial intelligence, and a host of other advancements, the perimeter has significantly deteriorated. It has been replaced with interconnected networks between partners, vendors, and even competitors in some cases involving blended programs and initiatives. This resulted in more complexity for corporate information technology (IT) networks, and complexity is the enemy of security.

Replacing the perimeter are other security risks such as third-party engagements, misconfiguration in cloud computing, application/digital vulnerabilities, and improper identity and access management, to name a few, and each will be covered in more detail in this book.

The deterioration of the perimeter is a clear example for directors that each business decision resulting in more partnerships, as well as technological advancements that require leveraging third-party networks, means the cyber security risks of those decisions will increase and will need to be addressed.

KNOW THY ENEMY

Often when we think of an adversary, a faceless entity that is almost myth-like or untouchable may come to mind. They hide behind malicious code and operate in the dark recesses of a hideout. In reality, there are different types of malicious actors, each with varying levels of sophistication and motives. I have seen first-hand evidence of their hands on, interactive reactions to our response and in one case, I was in the same room with a hacker after their arrest for a large data breach. The adversary is very much a real person.

It is important to realize that the adversaries are human, capable of decision-making, as well as employing tactics. They are motivated and hide behind the anonymity of the Internet from all corners of the globe. They are not theoretical or absent from reality.

What follows is a very general overview of the type of adversaries that operate across the globe. I refer to these in very broad groups, realizing that there are distinctions to each of the categories and my list may not be a complete one. The goal of this section is not only to explain that all adversaries have unique motivations, skill levels, and organizational make-up, but also to explain it at a high level for your general needs to understand in carrying out your director duties. There are threat intelligence groups across many different organizations and security companies that can do a much better job of providing more detail into these adversarial types than I do within these pages.

1. At the top of the adversarial heap is what the security industry calls advanced persistent threat (APT) or nation-state actors. These are well funded, motivated, and nation-state-sponsored actors who can be extremely organized. These groups can function as mission-oriented teams with a division of labor, each team with a specific task to achieve, and when completed, the next team moves in to perform their task. APT groups often operate using stealth, gaining occupancy in a network for extended periods of time without being noticed. Whether it is merger and acquisition data, strategic plans, research and development, or other trade secrets, APT actors focus their efforts on specific objectives. Often, they will use custom malware, specifically designed for the engagement, to break into the network. These adversaries may often be quiet in their endeavors, not wanting to be noticed.

2. Criminals and criminal groups are very active in cyber breaches with the goal of hacking for profit, in whatever form that takes (i.e., stealing financial data/credit card numbers, ransomware activities, stealing personal data for more customized phishing attacks in the future, or possibly selling malicious code). Some of these criminal groups are organized, or the attack could come from a lone criminal; there are many different levels of criminals with varying levels of sophistication within this category.

3. Hacktivists are hackers that seek to cause disruption through various attacks that may often be noisy, such as a corporate website deface-ment or a denial-of-service attack.[2] Their motivation is frequently related to social, religious, or political issues, specifically when corporate, government, or country initiatives are opposed to their beliefs. Examples may include climate issues, politics, human rights, or anti-war.

4. Another category of adversary is the stereotypical hacker that may be a lone person with motivations that span across financial gain, disruption, or theft of data. Potentially it could be a group of hackers, loosely or tightly organized, working together to meet their objective. For this adversarial group, the specific motivations and skill levels can vary greatly. Some may be called "script kiddies" who may not have a high level of hacking skill and rely on purchasing malware created by more advanced hackers to carry out their objective. Others could have significant expertise in carrying out their attacks.

5. The final group I will highlight in this chapter is referred to as insider threat. Our trusted employees have varying levels of access to sensitive corporate information, and as a result, are capable of causing significant harm to the organization. Insider threat can take (at a minimum) three forms: malicious, intentionally unauthorized, and accidental. A malicious example could be a disgruntled employee

who sabotages systems or steals corporate data to share or sell to competitors. Some employees may download large amounts of corporate data when leaving the company without the intent to sell to competitors, but the action still equates to an intentional and unauthorized act. Lastly, employees may cause disruption or data leakage without intent to cause harm or perform an unauthorized behavior. Instead, accidental actions by the employee, perhaps clicking on a link in a phishing email for example, can lead to grave damage to the company.

To the degree that corporations dedicate time to their business model, our adversaries are doing the same, leveraging a huge unsavory market opportunity to conduct business. Important for the director to understand is that many of the threat actor groups are not loosely based; they have strong business models with revenue-sharing opportunities related to providing unauthorized access via an access broker.

Companies are conducting business in new ways to increase top line revenue growth and improve bottom line efficiencies. The antiquated perimeter model of security is eroding to allow for more integrated partnerships. At the same time, our adversaries are growing their capabilities and tactics to launch attacks on any vulnerable corporation. Cyber insurance rates are climbing to historic levels and have become increasingly difficult to obtain. All of this makes for a perfect blend to raise cyber security to the top of any corporate executive's attention. Not surprisingly, cyber security is often included as one of the top threats for a corporation in their enterprise risk management program.

This section has painted a dismal view for corporations and my intent is to not fill the reader with fear, uncertainty, and doubt. Instead, it is to provide a realistic view into the threat landscape, while the rest of the book dives into areas where you can investigate within your corporate information security programs to reduce online risk.

Notes

1 Dark Web – the deep part of the Internet and chat rooms where criminals conduct commerce and exchange malicious content.
2 Denial of service is an attack whereby the adversary floods the targeted system/network with system traffic until the targeted system/network cannot respond to each request and then crashes, making the system unavailable for legitimate users.

Chapter 2

The chief information security officer role

With the many threat variables outlined in Chapter 1, a dedicated resource to organize and address those threats across multiple security disciplines is critical for corporations today. The role of chief information security officer (CISO) has been in place (in some capacity) for a few decades but is still considered by many to be a relatively new role. It is typically the highest position dedicated to cyber security for a corporation and is responsible for the information security program. Due to the constant evolution of the position, as well as the public awareness to the continued onslaught of cyberattacks, it does indeed feel like a young role to many. In fact, while the number of CISO appointments continues to grow, not all companies have a CISO role. As a result, we live in an exciting time within our industry insofar as we have front row seats in witnessing the evolution of this unique executive position – and perhaps even have a hand in evolving it ourselves.

In several cases, the role developed many years ago as breaches were increasing and regulatory issues were emerging, triggering a need for a leader to take point on information security. The logical choice was to appoint a person who deeply understood cyber security and was involved in the program. As a result, many technical persons who may not have possessed the core competencies in business administration, but had significant technical knowledge in cyber, were tapped for the responsibility. The new role then typically reported to the chief information officer (CIO) a mature executive role that balanced technology with business acumen and who could translate technology risks to senior management on behalf of the CISO. While the reporting structure for the CISO has evolved over the years, it still is a source of considerable debate in the security industry.

When considering a reporting structure for your CISO, it may not prove very effective to benchmark industry trends or what other corporations are doing because the structure is vastly different across companies. There are CISOs who report to the board, some to the chief executive officer

DOI: 10.1201/9781003477341-4

(CEO), general counsel, the chief financial officer (CFO), chief operating officer (COO), or as previously mentioned, the CIO. The straight answer on where the role should report is "it depends". What works for some companies may not be good for others. Traditionally the role reported to the CIO, but in recent years we've seen many CISO's transitioning out of IT due to (in part) a perceived conflict of interest with the leader responsible for establishing open and business-enabling technologies, also leading the function that secures those technologies. There may be a case in which the CIO, who is incentivized to produce technology capabilities for the company, funds such technologies over security budget increases which do not have the same immediate value visibility as productivity investments. Additionally, the field of cyber security has widened so significantly over the past decade; it becomes increasingly difficult for the CIO to stay abreast of the security field while maintaining their core competencies in understanding and delivering the multitude of business technology solutions.

Some in the industry say that placing a CISO as a direct report to the CEO demonstrates the company's dedication and support to the information security program. By aligning security with the highest level of corporate leadership, the message sent to employees is that information security is so vital to the company; direct oversight by the CEO is required to stay aligned to its progress.

Whatever the current argument within the industry related to reporting structure, the simple driver for deciding where to put the CISO in the org chart is simply around *access to leaders*. If the CISO has the ability to approach senior leaders with risk-based concerns and is able to present to you, the director, on a regular basis, reporting structure can be a moot point.

In my career, I have reported to CFOs, CIOs, general counsels, a CEO, and executive vice presidents of shared services. There was no single case where the security program was more effective because of my reporting structure. What made the programs successful was my ability to convey important matters of security in an unbiased, unfiltered forum for the highest levels of corporate leadership to make risk-based decisions. However, there is a need to ensure that the CISO is organizationally well established within the company, so they are seen as a peer to other senior executives leading other important functions.

Due to the importance of cyber security and its impact on the corporation, the role of CISO should be elevated to that of a senior executive in the corporation, and this would rely on the need for the CISO to have significant business expertise to excel in the position.

An interesting benchmark to understand how the CISO role is sometimes perceived is to browse job postings by companies or recruiting agencies searching for a CISO (look online for yourself). What follows are a few actual job requirements I have found for a few CISO positions over the past year:

- Significant practical, hands-on knowledge of the following:
  - packet analysis tools such as tcpdump, Wireshark, and ngrep
  - database structures and queries
  - Cisco or Palo Alto firewall/IPS administration
- Expertise with UNIX, Linux, Windows operating systems
- Hands-on experience with computer forensic investigation tools to collect, analyze, and preserve electronic evidence.
- Working knowledge and practical application of security products (both on-prem and cloud) including firewalls, vulnerability detection, network devices, endpoint protection, application testing, etc.
- Network security architecture development
- Degree in Software Development/Programming

CISO requirements such as these do little to advance the role to that of a peer executive in business and solidifies the long trend of thinking that the CISO is a technical position that administers technical controls and should report to another executive who has business experience and can translate it into corporate risk. It is true that some companies and recruiters do indeed understand the concept of what a true CISO should be; however, there is a clear opportunity to grow the role through education and challenging corporate leaders to the fact that an information security executive should be more focused on business risk than configuring firewall rule sets.

Absent from the above job description requirements are significant competencies in finance, strategy, operations, human resources, legal, marketing, and above all else, leadership. All of which are vital to perform as an effective CISO. The deep, hands-on, daily job skills within security operations are crucial; however, they are crucial for other roles within the cyber security organization – not the CISO.

Some industry colleagues may disagree with my addition of strong business qualifications in a CISO job description, explaining that the role should primarily have substantial expertise in information security; after all, information security is indeed in the job's title. I agree that the addition of business qualifications in the role should not dilute the need for cyber security expertise. It is a vital part of success for the CISO, so I am not inferring that business competencies replace cyber security skills. Moreover, when I refer to business skills in the above domains, I am not suggesting a casual understanding of these skills. Instead, I believe the CISO should have deep expertise in these business domains, as much as any other "C-level" executive that holds a leadership position across finance, operations, HR, or strategy.

What makes the CISO role so challenging is the need for having deep technical underpinnings, expertise in managing risk, an understanding of attack tactics, their response measures, strategic security planning, *and* all the aforementioned business requirements, to make for an effective leader. Some of these skills, for example, incident response or technical expertise, lie dormant until they need to be leveraged in an exceptional situation. But the core business and leadership proficiencies are always there on the surface, used every day.

For at least ten years within the cyber security industry, I have read or heard about the need for the CISO to "have a seat at the table" when it comes to discussions with the board of directors for corporations. It is a perennial discussion that desperately requires substance over a mere rally cry. What lacks in the debate are concrete examples of *how* CISO's achieve this seat. Many will say that it has positively evolved, with many CISOs now presenting to the board multiple times per year, so progress has been made – which is indeed a positive trend for our role and our industry. But make no mistake, while there are many corporations that have invited CISOs to the boardroom on their own accord, many have not done so out of some transformational evolution of all CISOs speaking to the business aspects of cyber security. In reality, it was only because of regulatory requirements or industry pressure based on the onslaught of breaches that forced us to be there. Had it not been for these external pressures to have cyber security discussed at the board level, many CISOs would still be vacant from the boardroom. It is (long past) time for CISOs to proactively alter our destiny through less debate on *why* the role should have a seat at the table and demonstrate core competencies of *how* we can be drawn into the boardroom, rather than be regulated or pressured to be there.

One positive outcome of the pressures to include cyber security more broadly across the business is awareness of the topic itself. Never in my career have I seen such interest or enthusiasm to learn more about our industry and the threats that impact all of us. Capitalizing on this opportunity requires more than just knowledge of cyber security; what a simple role it would be if we only had to recite common risks and potential countermeasures. What differentiates an effective CISO is the ability to understand these common risks and potential countermeasures, and then weave them into the business environment to which the CISO is delivering services. To do this requires a deep understanding of the business in which they belong, and to accomplish this understanding, a strong knowledge of all business domains is required. And this entire process takes time. It is nearly impossible to do this in a one-year tenure at an organization and unfortunately the tenure for many CISO's is not as long as other executives.

Many factors contribute to some of the high turnover in the CISO role. It is a high-stress position in which the executive must be ready to act at a moment's notice equating to very little down time. In their work, the adversaries only have to be right one time while the CISO and their staff need to be correct every time. It is much more difficult to be in a constant cyber-defensive posture rather than the offensive position of our adversaries. There are large numbers of disciplines within cyber security that force the CISO to be attentive to multiple initiatives across a broad spectrum. In some cases, they may feel as if they are unable to initiate change in reducing risk given the culture of their new company. All these factors can lead to burnout and may have influence on the short tenure for many CISOs.

To find a truly effective CISO, it is worth looking at the average tenure of past CISO roles that each of your candidates possesses. A successful CISO will have several years of average tenure at the companies in which they've worked. Careers are dependent upon a number of factors, and it is common to have perhaps one CISO tenure for a candidate lasting only one year, sprinkled in with other roles lasting several years. For example, a CISO may have worked for a company that they found to be less supportive of security initiatives than expected. Or perhaps after starting, the new executive realizes the financial posture of the company isn't as strong as anticipated. The CISO should alleviate some of this risk during the interview process by asking direct questions related to corporate culture surrounding information security, or perhaps more deeply researching the company's Annual and 10-K reports for information on free operating cash flow, debt, and other financial triggers pointing to the current financial posture. Regardless, there may be circumstances which, even with strong pre-hire research, the CISO finds themselves in a situation outside of their control which requires them to move on after just a year in the position. Therefore, it is imperative that senior leadership looks at the *overall* average tenure and strongly considers those with a higher average of successful years to move forward in the selection process.

Those CISOs who consistently move from company to company after only one year may possess strong security strategy development skills, but they will lack the critical competencies of *executing* a strategic plan over time. Without the experience of implementation, feeling the struggles of applying a strategy and working through conflict, the candidate will not be as successful as their peers. A good CISO has the scar tissue from past execution experiences.

Exploring a CISO candidate's execution experience is also a good way to investigate how they go about staggered implementations. Does the candidate strive to do more with less resources as the funding is delivered incrementally, or do they wait until full funding has been provided prior to executing a plan? Answers to these questions may be indicators to how successful the candidate will be during a potentially challenging funding period.

CISO OPTIONS

Another popular trend for companies is to outsource the CISO role to a security company that provides virtual chief information security officer (vCISO) services. Akin to a consultant, the vCISO provides fractional or part-time security leadership services to a company so the customer can avoid the cost of a full-time equivalency (FTE) CISO. Aside from the proposed cost savings, the benefit of such a service may be marketed as the vCISO having good visibility into risks across multiple clients and industries and can then weave that knowledge into security strategies for your company. Along with the senior leaders of the company, you should closely evaluate the use of vCISO services to ensure it is the right choice for the business.

As regulations increase and with cyber breaches on the rise, outsourcing such a critical role could prove problematic. Even if your company is very small, it doesn't eliminate the risk of intrusion (recall that ransomware leveled the threat playing field for corporations of all sizes and industries). Additionally, the wide view of what other clients are doing in security is not likely to apply to every company since each one has such unique needs and risk postures.

While many vCISO companies provide excellent services, an investigation into the overall vCISO industry will show more than a few examples of vCISO's with little or no CISO experience. Persons with a desire to break into the CISO role may start by creating a limited liability company (LLC) for a few hundred dollars to provide vCISO services to clients but they lack the hands-on, past experience of holding a dedicated CISO role for a corporation. Outsourcing security services in general is not a negative strategy; later in this book, we will examine a few examples where outsourcing other portions of the security service catalog may make good financial sense. Like with any decision to proxy a critical portion of your business externally, deep analysis must be done to ensure it is the correct strategic plan for the company.

CISO SELECTION PROCESS

Due to the criticality of the role, it is important for members of the board of directors to be involved in creating the criteria, as well as the selection process, for the CISO position. The depth of that involvement is up to each unique board. At one company in my career, the board helped to create the distinguishing competencies that the CISO should possess. In other cases, the third-party auditor assisted the board in building the selection criteria for the role in which I was awarded. And with one company, one of my final interviews was with the chairman of the technology committee of the board. We each flew to a central airport, met in the conference room of an airline club, and spoke for three hours. While this level of involvement is extraordinary, it provided me with a preliminary close look into the security culture of the board, at the same time giving the committee chair a view into how I approached security. Additionally, it jump-started the relationship, which served valuable in my time at the company.

There are several core competencies and traits that should be examined in CISO candidates. Above all else, trust in your new CISO is a key component for an effective relationship. It is understood that trust isn't something that is easily drawn out in the interview process and takes time to build, but it is a key differentiator for what makes the CISO a successful one. Trust can be better measured by directors by engaging early and often with the candidate, and this could start with the interview process.

The importance of business administration skills has been covered in the previous section but the criticality of these skills for a CISO to effectively perform in the role bear repeating. A CISO candidate should be able to discuss various business-related topics during the interview process that speak to the specific underpinnings of the financial posture for the company that they are pursuing. Conveying a deep understanding of the corporate makeup, leadership, top revenue-generating business units, as well any challenges the business is facing, is a good signal for you that the candidate can understand the business aspects of the company. Moreover, candidates who also intertwine that knowledge specific to your business with cyber security implications could be a very viable prospect. They won't get it one hundred percent accurate by leveraging solely external data, but the thought process used by the candidate is a great indicator of potential success.

You obviously desire that the potential CISO has expertise in cyber security, but not at the expense of the business. A truly secure computer is one that is turned off and unplugged. But in order to conduct business, solid risk management choices must be made in securing the infrastructure. Some historic CISO mindsets of consistently saying "no" to business initiatives have been replaced with approaches that deliver business goals, but in a customized and secure way. Ensuring that this new wave of thinking resides in your candidates is critically important, and the best way to draw this out is through examples and scenarios.

Provide your applicant with business scenarios that highlight their views on risk management. These scenarios should be based on issues needing complex decisions without overtly correct or incorrect choices. An example of a poor scenario would be for the candidate to describe their views between a company patching system vulnerabilities, or not interfering with the business and allowing the systems to go unpatched for an extended period of time as long as they are documented. Instead, choose scenarios in which both choices may appear less than desirable. The key thing to look for in the candidates' answers goes beyond discussing high severity risks and their potential impact to the business. A well-qualified, business-oriented

CISO candidate will also examine the *likelihood* of a risk being realized in all of their decisions. In business strategy, it is usually the likelihood of a risk that will tilt a decision to move forward with a plan or to shelve it.

Emotional intelligence is an important attribute for all executives, and when it comes to CISOs, it could prove vital for the leader who is the one between your company and the adversaries. One of the most important attributes the role demands is remaining calm across multiple scenarios. The ability to identify and regulate our emotions (and those of others) as we navigate through the day as a security executive, whatever happiness or challenge it may bring, helps the CISO to be optimally effective. When a CISO is calm and assured, they can better identify with the feelings of others and make more empathetic decisions. Their ability to understand the different needs of the stakeholders, and those of the team, will help the CISO to consider all angles of an issue, which leads to more impactful decisions. The CISO can then make solid choices without allowing personal needs or emotions to cloud the decision.

During a response to an incident, you need to know that the CISO is stable, calm, and focused on the response. A CISO who is excited and emotional can transfer these traits to their team. I've heard it called "having a steady heart rate". Whatever description is chosen, a CISO who remains calm during the storm instills confidence in the responders that their leader is focused, and everything will ultimately be okay.

Like the team, the adversary is closely watching, but their intent is to look for clues on the response. Does the CISO perform knee jerk, reactive tasks? If so, it may tip their hand to the adversary who will inevitably fold up tents and move somewhere else in the network, adding delays to the response. It is much better for the security executive to follow normal processes while they work up a response that is calm and measured.

Whether it be times of great excitement and exhilaration, or intense frustration, the true security leader will work to identify and control their emotions to be maximally effective and to convey confidence to their team. You should seek out methods to understand and gauge the emotional intelligence of your CISO candidates.

While there are many desired qualifications for your next CISO, the last one I will highlight is communication. A candidate who can translate complex technologies and security jargon into easy-to-understand concepts that aid in effective business decisions is no longer a nice to have trait; it is the baseline. We all have varying levels of understanding on different topics and cyber security is no different. Your search should begin and end with CISO candidates who can advise the board succinctly and effectively, no matter the board's cyber fluency.

My undergraduate degree is in philosophy with an interest in ethics. One of the domains in that course of study was communicative ethics, which goes beyond obvious things like truth telling and maintaining confidentiality. The discipline emphasizes our duty as communicators and listeners. Communication consists of an originator and a receiver of a message. The duty for clear and effective communication, ensuring the message is understood by the audience, lies with the originator. The discipline states that it is unethical to waste the receiver's time and energy with unclear communication.

Exceptional CISO candidates will demonstrate the ability to convey their message in such a way that it makes it easy for a listener of all skill levels to make solid business decisions. In other words, they understand the requirement for clear communication lies squarely on themselves. My approach to communicating a security strategy to an executive management team involves several conversations. If I know that I will be presenting my proposal to the CEO in the near future, I'll create several versions of the strategic plan and have conversations with different members of the CEO's direct staff.

I will meet with the chief HR officer to discuss the labor aspects of my plan, outlining the critical skill sets needed for the security team, our skill gaps, and the number of FTEs I will need to execute the plan. We discuss training, geographic regions where I will be placing employees, and why the choice of regions provides value to the strategy. There is a conversation about the industry gap in well-qualified security experts and how I plan to address it. Perhaps we will discuss internships or potentially cross training employees from different departments on cyber security disciplines. At the end of the meeting, the CHRO completely understands the HR elements of the security plan.

Next, I move to a one-on-one discussion with the CFO to discuss the financial aspects of my strategy. We focus on which initiatives can be capitalized and which are operating expense. Also important in this conversation are when each initiative will hit the budget in the fiscal year and what can be delayed. I highlight the labor costs as well as technology costs, with an explanation of what I plan to outsource and what will be built in-house.

One of the final conversations is with the CIO in which we discuss the technology attributes of the strategy. How can we leverage existing technology partnerships and what capabilities need to be added to fill a gap? We explore how my proposed technologies will interact with currently deployed IT technologies or perhaps the potential latency impacts to systems as a result of an added security technology on top of it.

As a result of these preliminary discussions, when the presentation for the CEO and his or her direct reports takes place in which I walk through the strategy, there are many nodding heads of affirmation by the CEO's team. They say, "Yes, I've seen the plan and am good with it". The outcome is the CEO is in a better position to make a decision because the decision-making process was made easy for them. Regardless of the process the candidate uses in examples during the interview conversations, you should seek out those candidates who communicate in such a way to make the decisions flow more easily.

CISO ACCOUNTABILITY

Many industry examples exist in which the CISO is fired after a cyber breach at the company in which they led the security program. Putting factors of unethical or illegal activities aside, this practice should be considered carefully by the directors and the management team before the decision is made. First, companies should embrace the concept that security is everyone's responsibility. Each employee, no matter the department in which they perform their duties, has a role to play in ensuring the company is secure. The entire landscape of potential incubators of compromise for a corporation should not fall on one person's shoulders. While it is true that the CISO is indeed accountable for developing, maintaining, and operational oversight of the cyber security program, breaches still occur no matter how many preventative controls are implemented.

Human error from a sales representative or perhaps a project manager by clicking on a malicious link in a phishing email and entering their credentials so that the attacker can gain access is just one example of how security controls can be bypassed. A CISO who successfully implements robust security technologies, optimal processes, and supplements them with detailed security awareness training, should not be terminated for one instance of human error by one employee, especially after these technology and administrative controls have been effectively deployed. Comparatively, we rarely see CFOs fired when a single employee steals funds from the company. Nor do we see COOs terminated when a piece of manufacturing equipment is damaged due to improper maintenance by one service technician employee. The scale of these two examples could vary greatly, but the core theory is that individual activities (both incidental and by accident) can cost the company significantly. Executives across the C-suite create and oversee programs with preventive controls, coupled with detection processes for identifying anomalies from standard thresholds and the ability to respond to incidents expediently. But the negative impacts due to the acts of one employee can (and often do) still take place.

Perhaps an argument to the examples I use above is to say that a cyber security breach financially impacts the corporation significantly more than a person stealing funds from the company or shutting down production due to inadequate servicing of equipment. I would challenge that argument by looking at the number of historical examples involving corporate theft as well as manufacturing mishaps, but nevertheless, let's explore this argument a bit more. If we terminate one executive due to the actions of another person who circumvented a control (with or without intent) because the financial impact is so great but at the same time do not fire another executive using the same example details except the financial impact was not materially impactful, this introduces a few issues. Using this logic, what is the financial threshold, that specific financial figure, that says any executive who's financial loss impact is below that figure is safe, but any executive who's financial impact is above that financial amount is terminated? There isn't, nor should there be such a financial threshold.

Sticking with this example just a bit longer, I believe the scale of responsibility should be evaluated. In the manufacturing example, not every employee has access to the manufacturing floor, and even fewer are service technicians capable of causing disruption. In the finance example, not every employee has access to money or to financial systems that provides a better than average opportunity to steal. But with cyber security, the number of employees capable of causing disruption is not as limited – every employee with access to a computer and email account can be sent phishing emails, social engineered on the telephone, insert an infected USB drive into a work computer, or fall for any number of risks. Moreover, the employee can be breached on their personal device/account, outside of work, which may carry over into the corporate infrastructure.

The true effectiveness of a program lies in the preventative controls implemented, the ability to detect potential issues, and how robust the response capabilities are in the wake of an issue so that the business can return to normal operations. If such a program is in place and due diligence was achieved, the executive has performed their due care.

Next, an effective CISO brings risks to leadership and advises on suggested strategies to mitigate those risks. Through executive decisions, or perhaps through an Information Security Steering committee made up of corporate executives, the CISO does not ultimately make the choice whether to invest in a risk mitigating process/technology on their own. Senior executives are the approvers of budget and allocate funds across the company. Effective security is a team endeavor, each one playing a vital role.

Lastly, firing a CISO after a breach can be short sighted. I attend several information security conferences over the course of a year; it is a valuable chance to learn from industry peers and service providers on how to thwart the latest threats. After the keynotes are completed, attendees move to various breakout sessions, each one focusing on a different topic. The sessions that talk about general risks are usually the sessions that attendees can easily find a chair to settle into and listen to the speaker. Finding a seat in sessions that talk about specific methodologies that a CISO successfully deployed is a bit more difficult. But those sessions with a CISO speaker outlining the lessons learned from a recent large breach are always standing room only. Everyone wants to learn more about those nuggets of information that they can take back to their companies and fold them into their security program.

Why terminate this CISO with all that real-life knowledge of incident response, only to watch them go to another company to apply those lessons learned? Additionally, the company spends money to hire, onboard, and acclimate a new replacement CISO who must learn about the breach from an outsider perspective and start all over with their own strategy. Also of note is that the security industry is a close-knit bunch, and word of a post-breach CISO termination by a company is widely shared. Finding an exceptional CISO to replace the former one may prove difficult for a corporation if it has a reputation for firing security executives after a breach.

Of course, all these aforementioned considerations are moot if the CISO engages in unethical, fraudulent, illegal, or other activities that display a lack of regard in their duties.

GIVING UP ON THE CISO ROLE

As I write this, there are a few industry articles discussing the need to re-evaluate the CISO role due to its perceived failure. Failure in its evolution and planning, failure in its transition to be looked upon as a peer executive, and failure to align its focus outside of solely operational initiatives. Many authors of these posts mention the difficulty in finding CISOs who possess strong business experience in addition to the cyber security expertise needed. High stress, short tenures, and CISO accountability issues in the wake of breaches are also mentioned – all topics we've explored together earlier in this chapter. To alleviate these concerns, some argue the industry should come to terms that the CISO role failed and look for alternatives to address cyber risk among corporations. For the most part, I agree with all of these authors about the history and the issues that have arose with the CISO role as it matured. It is natural to have growing pains. Where our opinions differ is the manner in which we should address the matter. Rather than call for the demise of the role at the same time as regulatory requirements and breaches increase – my focus is to enhance the role through awareness, feedback loops, and creating an environment in which the role can add even more value.

Proponents for moving the CISO role down a few organizational levels and re-focusing it on technical issues may suggest a different role to elevate to the executive team: the chief security officer (CSO), chief risk officer (CRO), or something similar. This role would lead a cross-functional team of cyber security, physical (corporate) security, risk management, business continuity, and perhaps privacy. With this model, the executive is now responsible for even *more* initiatives than the CISO, with the expectation that having more programs to oversee would somehow allow for increased adoption of the role by executive teams. I see the opposite happening: a dilution of focus on cyber security by adding more functions. Cyber security is much too important for our companies to move it down the organizational chart. I have served as a CSO for two corporations; additionally, I have seen how the disciplines of cyber security, corporate security, business continuity, and privacy are addressed in many other corporations. While they are all very important areas of the business and absolutely should collaborate between one another, cyber security frequently has the most risk velocity among them. For smaller companies, the physical security (non-cyber security) functions often are expertly led at the director and manager levels.

At enormous organizations, the roles of cyber security, corporate security, and privacy may be split across three executives (often vice president level) due to the extraordinarily complex work each was performing. The bottom line for how to organize all security-related functions is dependent on the nature and criticality for each of the domains for that particular company. But in no case have I seen productive suggestions where the CISO role diminishing in scope provides a solution to elevate the importance of cyber security in an organization.

As a technology industry, we've seen other roles marked for extinction as well. Going back ten plus years, more than a few consultancies discussed the demise of the CIO role, the top executive responsible for the information technology program, replacing it with other roles. A decade later, the CIO role is still a prominent role across executive leadership teams.

Filling a critical role like the CISO takes strong engagement by the management team and board of directors, with some potential assistance from external professional service providers. The time invested in researching and drawing out the needed attributes for a CISO among your candidate pool will provide large dividends. A popular saying that I never grow tired of hearing is "always do something today that your future self will thank you for".

Chapter 3

Security vs. compliance

It is important for me to begin this chapter by stating that compliance to regulatory requirements is of the utmost importance and I would never suggest that adherence to them is a wasted effort. With that said, I believe that there is a vast difference in compliance and security, with many opportunities to enhance the way corporate governance boards view compliance as it relates to cyber security. More to the point, one only needs to look at the typical board committee that discusses security, traditionally the audit committee (more on this later). Security is often viewed as a compliance or audit issue rather than what it could be viewed as a business risk issue with deep technological underpinnings.

At first glance, bundling information security into compliance seems to make sense, after all, they are typically bound by similar topical areas. For example, reviewing effectiveness in user access reviews by the external auditor does indeed relate to the identity and access management domain in security. Another reason for combining the two is that packaging security into compliance is much easier when it comes to audit remediation. If I present a business case to management for approval and I tag on the statement, "this will address one of our audit items", the approval process will typically be easier for me. That is because, in part, the audit item involves a project that has a start, a middle, and a finish. One can see, and measure, the adherence to a specific finding until its completion. With information security, there often isn't such a clean process; even after implementing a project that deploys a security technology or process, a breach may still occur. Among all the content within this book, this is the most critical statement worth remembering: information security is not a project, instead, it is a program that requires constant nurturing and adjustments to make it effective – it has no completion date.

For example, perhaps there is an audit finding that says there should be a security control such as a data loss prevention (DLP) technology deployed across the company. That audit project starts with the finding that no DLP solution exists within the company to protect against sensitive data leakage.

The report provides details of the failure and recommends that management should deploy a DLP solution, along with dates and responsible parties for its implementation. There is a beginning, a middle, and an end to this project, and each month, the teams meet to discuss progress on the audit finding. Once the DLP solution is installed, the spirit of the audit finding has been met and the audit finding is closed. If only cyber security were as easy as this.

Now suppose the implementation of that same DLP solution was done by simply identifying the best DLP platform on the market, partnering with a technology vendor, receiving approval (which comes a bit easier because it is an audit issue), working through the procurement cycle, and installing the DLP technology. No configuration was done in deploying the solution; it merely reports on the number of data leakage incidents occurring but does not block those transmissions. No data classification program has been put in place for the company, nor has there been an inventory of what types of sensitive data exist in the company or where they reside. The company merely installed a DLP solution with factory settings. The audit requirement was fulfilled, but the core security issues pertaining to unauthorized data transmissions still exist.

As another example, suppose a user has access to the Enterprise Resource Planning (ERP) solution for the enterprise, but the employee leaves the company. External auditors identify that the employee retained access to the ERP solution even after leaving the company. As a result of further investigation, they realize that network access, along with remote access capabilities, was indeed removed from the user effectively and in a timely manner. Auditors may say that because the employee could not access the network and traverse to the ERP solution where residual access remains, no audit finding exists. However, as companies move to more Software as a Service (SaaS) solutions, which may not require corporate network access, the ability to login to those SaaS solutions still presents a security issue at the application level. Both cases highlight the difference in compliance and security, and both of these are real-life scenarios I have seen often in my career. Good compliance does not equate to good security, but good security can be helpful in showing good compliance.

In 2019, I contributed content to the book, *CISO Compass* by Todd Fitzgerald.[1] In it, my article called "The Colonoscopy of Cyber Security" further details the differences between cyber security and compliance using a life insurance example. Comparing the limited medical screening done on behalf of the insurance carrier, to my full medical exam completed by my primary physician, I conclude that both medical screenings seek to accomplish the same thing: a determination of my health. But both do so for very different reasons. The same holds true between compliance and security insofar as they both seek to identify a security posture, but they attempt to accomplish this for different reasons.

THE COST OF COMPLIANCE

So far, this chapter has focused on the theoretical challenges with bundling compliance with information security, but there are operational and financial considerations as well. In addressing compliance issues (which again are of the utmost importance), the remediation is primarily focused on clearing the administrative audit finding itself and may not contribute to solving the root cause within security that may have initiated the finding. Significant resources and attention are dedicated to audit remediation, and it is not uncommon to assemble a large, multi-departmental team to devote substantial time in addressing a significant finding. Not absent from this team is the chief information security officer (CISO) and many team members from their security organization. Obviously, the CISO and their security team's contributions are necessary in addressing compliance issues. However, could there be such a thing as too much lower-value involvement from the CISO in addressing audit finding remediation, particularly in activities that don't require substantial cyber security expertise?

When a CISO is embedded in compliance activities, they are pulled away from cyber security initiatives, perhaps even those initiatives that could prevent another similar audit finding in the future. Some common audit findings with security implications may fall under user access reviews and not obtaining evidence in the form of documented approvals by managers for permitting access to one (or more) of the employees on their team to a particular application. Resolving an active finding includes going to the managers multiple times and requesting that they approve, or show evidence of approval, for the access, each attempt done through email requests or physically going to the manager to request the approval. It may be an issue in which the manager doesn't understand the technical jargon used within a platform that explains what entitlements are given at specific access levels. If this is the case, the CISO and security team work to provide education to the manager(s) on the various levels of access. Administrative tasks such as tracking and chasing down approvals or manually clarifying the various access levels are now being done by cyber security professionals, which the company is highly compensating them for to provide specialized security services in an industry with limited resources. But in this case, they are not performing those specialized services and instead are doing more time-consuming administrative type work and at a higher rate of compensation.

Because compliance and information security are two different disciplines, as well as the notion that remediating specific compliance findings may not lend itself to solving the root cause of the finding, it seems appropriate that corporate leadership teams and directors thoughtfully consider if bundling security and compliance activities into one organization makes good business sense for the company. Through detailed demand management inquiries on the amount of time a CISO is involved in remediation activities, as well as the labor costs for the CISO and their team to work on compliance, leadership may conclude that combining the two disciplines may not be optimally effective or financially value added for their specific corporation. It may be determined that a project manager, IT analyst, or similar role could facilitate the administrative work of remediating an audit finding, providing needed time for the security team to focus on countermeasures that will help prevent similar, future audit findings. In other cases, the financial impact could prove to be immaterial. Either way, the cost of compliance can and should be evaluated and controlled for maximum effectiveness.

Compliance is just one critical component for corporate success and requires deep oversight by the board of directors and/or a board committee. In Chapter 4, we'll review the board structure as it relates to cyber security for a more detailed view into potential opportunities to enhance it.

Note

1 Todd Fitzgerald, *CISO Compass: Navigating Cybersecurity Leadership Challenges with Insights from Pioneers*. Auerbach CRC Press, 2019, pp. 15–16.

Examining the information security board governance structure

The manner in which a CISO presents to their board of directors is as unique as the information security program for the company itself. Yet, there are some general themes that can be garnered from industry research into how a CISO reports to the board (or a committee). In today's current environment, it is not uncommon for a majority of CISOs to present to a board committee, with many of these presentations provided to the audit committee.

The inclusion of cyber security as an agenda item at the board level is a critical success factor for corporate governance and something that has significantly improved in the past decade. There is no better way for you to understand what the company is undertaking to combat cyber threats than by receiving regular updates from your CISO several times each year.

The frequency of board-level cyber updates varies from company to company, but a typical cadence for my career has been quarterly updates. In some cases, the CISO presents to a committee for three consecutive quarters, with a full board briefing in one quarter (perhaps in Q1 or Q4 for an annual review type of briefing).

The audit committee has historically been the home for cyber security updates to directors. Whatever the previous reasons for placing cyber security under the audit committee at these companies, it is time for boards to re-examine how cyber security issues are brought to their attention, as well as the committee structure used to bring forth those issues.

In my observations, audit committees are inundated with topical areas that reach across internal audit, external audit, information technology, cyber security, and with other areas being added every year. Covering all these topics in a single committee meeting means the agenda items are typically brief to allow for all topics to be covered. This is particularly true if there is, for example, a transformational digital implementation or movement to a new ERP solution for the IT organization. Or perhaps there are higher than normal internal or external audit activities taking place that require more attention from the committee. It appears that many in the industry agree, with various comments on the increased scope for audit committees surfacing in business articles.

Imagine (as an example) that the average information security briefing for a company is fifteen minutes on the committee's agenda each quarter. If accurate, it is my opinion that a total of one hour each year is not enough time for directors to understand, question, challenge, and provide guidance on important cyber security topics for the company, given today's environment. This *shortest hour* is one of the most critical for protecting a corporation, and it would be prudent for boards to re-examine the placement of cyber security within the audit committee to allow more attention to the topic and make any necessary adjustments based on their assessment.

In recent years, our industry has seen an increase of separation from cyber being discussed at the Audit Committee, moving instead to a Technology Committee, or in some cases (and with this author's belief of anticipated frequency of the practice in the future), a dedicated Cyber Security Committee. These companies have realized that technology is an increasingly important enabler to their business strategy and directors desire to have more understanding of the strategies incorporating these technologies. Aside from the benefits for CIOs and their IT organizations, a technology committee provides a well-structured forum for the CISO to discuss important cyber security topics. During my career, I have worked with just one Technology Committee amongst all the Boards and committees to which I presented. I found the experience to be valuable to the degree that more security initiatives could be discussed, and while we never dive into technical details at the board committee level, the structure did allow for more depth in areas such as strategic and operational oversight.

The emergence of dedicated cyber security committees is not out of the realm of possibility. In fact, there are predictions that more boards will have a dedicated cyber security committee in the not-so-distant future. Many factors contribute to the emergence of such a committee, not the least of which is the identification of cyber-related threats landing near the top of corporations' enterprise risk management programs. Additionally, at the time of this writing, new emerging regulations require companies to publicly divulge the details around their cyber security oversight. With more board attention to an area that is considered high risk for global corporations, the natural evolution of cyber-centric committees will follow.

BOARD ENGAGEMENTS

The level of interaction between the CISO and the board of directors varies widely due to the uniqueness of board make-up, industry, security posture of the company, and a host of other variables. There are different options available to the director for learning more about cyber security, specifically the posture and potential impacts for your organization.

No matter the board format, CISOs should weave into all presentations the positive things about the cyber security posture, as well as any negative gaps of coverage. It is always good to hear of the positive strides your company is taking in cyber security, but more importantly, you should understand the concerns of the security executive so remediation plans can be discussed. This seems intuitive, but having a process for drawing out such concerns can alleviate future misunderstandings. To accomplish this, I had committee chairpersons and other directors formally ask me, "Are you aware of any material gaps in the cyber program and do you currently have all of the resources you need for the company's cyber security program"? Such formality helps to promote an open conversation between the CISO and the director, as well as documenting the content in the committee/board minutes.

There are many typical interaction types between the CISO and the board, and those interactions may include the following.

FULL BOARD PRESENTATIONS

Gathering the entire board of directors for a cyber briefing is a great way to provide general industry news, the likelihood of risks for the corporation, and how the company might address those risks. Many CISOs have broad relationships across the security industry, and you should consider leveraging their relationships to enhance the full board presentations. Perhaps a briefing by the local office of the Federal Bureau of Investigation (FBI), Secret Service, or maybe a CEO from a top-rated cyber security company could enhance the awareness of cyber across the entire board?

Dependent upon committee scheduling, often in my career I have seen non-audit committee members of the board sit in on my committee cyber security briefings because of an interest in the topic. Expanding the audience to the full board for listening to general cyber topical areas can be quite valuable for all members of the team.

REGULAR CYBER BRIEFINGS

Whatever the committee structure or frequency of cyber updates that your board chooses, cyber security briefings on a regular cadence help to bring awareness to the company's security initiatives. It is important to remember that each briefing is not a standalone session, nor does it deliver merely a general overview of the program with some metrics. Instead, each briefing is just one chapter in a larger book that collectively tells the overall story of the company's security posture and its progressively increased ability to respond to threats.

This "installment-based" style of briefing perfectly suits a company that is building or significantly enhancing a cyber security program. The

CISO begins with a briefing on the assessment of the current security program, then highlights the strategic information security plan (with all its components) and how it will deliver risk-mitigating services. At subsequent briefings, the CISOs can discuss their progress in executing the strategic plan. Ultimately, each committee member will have a full view of where the company's security program was, the incremental success on the execution to the strategy, and a final view into how the investment areas of security to date have helped to reduce (not eliminate) the identified initial risks. All intertwined with the specific needs of the company.

This type of briefing on the progress to the overall strategy should not be a perennial presentation. A large transformation of the security program, building a new security program or hearing from a new CISO on their strategic plan, should be limited in frequency. If you are consistently being briefed on large, programmatic changes to the security organization, it could be a sign that the company is changing CISOs too frequently or perhaps previous security strategies may not have been thoroughly comprehensive. Of course, strategies are dynamic in nature and must adjust to evolving business models, as well as evolving threats. Instead, I refer more to large strategies that focus on building a security program where one minimally exists, or a new strategic plan that usually follows the appointment of a new CISO to the company. In these cases, I suggest that an underlying factor may be present which causes the frequent strategic plan briefings and is a factor that you should investigate.

Once an assessment and initial strategic plan briefing is completed and there is a transition to more steady-state briefings, the committee should hear of security topics that provide a solid understanding of current and upcoming risks based on corporate strategic adjustments, potential impacts to the company, security industry updates, as well as informative metrics. Every board will require unique metrics that assist them in their understanding of cyber and importantly how it relates to the company. Because each board is so unique, I like to ask the directors that I present to which specific metrics they would like to see. I supplement the requests with other security metrics that I feel are important for me to deliver. This "top-down, bottom-up" metrics strategy helps to provide insightful measurements for board members.

I've been challenged on the notion of asking board members what metrics they would like to see in their updates. More than a couple industry peers, as well as some leaders, told me that the board doesn't have the cyber knowledge to understand which metrics to ask for; the metrics should come from the CISO who understands the domain. I disagree with these challenges because metrics are used to make decisions and ensure proper oversight. Who better to know what data aids them in those decisions and oversight than the persons who actually perform the decision-making and oversight? I do not have the knowledge to design and build an automobile, but I can identify what is important to me and what I look for when purchasing a vehicle. I ask the car dealer about specific metrics/measurements of the vehicle, instead of just allowing him or her to tell me only what they feel I should know.

As for board members not having the cyber knowledge to request the appropriate metrics, well, that is the reason you and I are investing our time on this book – to provide a broad-based understanding of cyber security for the director. With this knowledge gained, you will be able to adequately highlight the metrics that are most important for you and the board. Lastly, my asking for their opinion on metrics I should provide does not eliminate me from providing my own metrics I feel are important. The combination of the two is more powerful than a one-way conversation.

Metrics which speak to a company's ability to detect and respond to threats, so that normal business operations can resume, are of the most interest. How long does it take for our security team to detect an incident? How fast can the team conduct triage activities to validate it is an actual issue for the company? How long does the collaboration across other departments take for the team to fully remediate the incident? These measurements speak to the heart of how fast the company can recover from an incident and resume normal business operations. The number of cyber security incidents or vulnerabilities per quarter, categorized by low, medium, high, and critical, may not provide the same level of actionable information for the committee. In fact, presenting such data may drive more confusion and questions than clarity. A security operations program can generate huge amounts of alerts, most of which are not relevant after deciphering between what are false positives[1] or perhaps what are legitimate business processes triggering the alert. The more that metrics facilitate decision-making the better, and it is up to every CISO to work with the board to determine exactly what those metrics are, so those decisions can be made. As mentioned previously, each board and security program are unique. Their metrics ought to be as well.

1:1 INTERACTIONS

There are times when a specific board member requires more specificity on the information security program. This can take a few different forms, dependent on the situation. For example, one of the directors may have significant technology, or better, cyber security expertise that they bring to the board dynamic. They may set up a recurring hour with the CISO to dive into the security program a bit deeper than what is covered in a committee or board briefing. Such a director will ask pointed questions about the protection of the company's payment card systems, or perhaps more information on how the security program specifically protects the corporation against ransomware. These interactions are a great way to explore more deeply the underpinnings of the cyber security program while keeping the committee briefings more broad based and results oriented in nature.

It was often the case when a new director was elected to the board, I was asked to brief them on the security program for the company where they were about to begin their duties. During my career there were many times when I would fly to a location and meet with the new director to provide this type of 1:1 briefing. Covering areas such as the security posture of the company, any residual risks that exist, the appropriateness of the security resources for the team, and top threats to the company are beneficial for the new director to understand. Additionally, it jump-starts the relationship between the CISO and the newest board member.

The interaction between the committee chairperson and the CISO should reflect the criticality of this important relationship. You have read about my previous job interview with the technology committee chairperson and the benefits for both of us during that interaction, but the conversations extended beyond that discussion. We would meet one-on-one prior to the committee meeting to discuss what I will presenting, but with more detail on the intent or backstory of the content. This was very helpful as it laid out the upcoming session for the chairperson, as well as provided me with critical feedback on areas I could expand upon in the committee briefing. Whatever form it takes, directors should take advantage of the CISO's knowledge to probe into more details on cyber security in an informal, one-on-one format.

INCIDENT RESPONSE BRIEFINGS

Several years ago, I had to make a very difficult Saturday morning phone call to the CEO of my company at the time. I notified him that a significant breach was taking place at our company, and we stood up the incident response team (supplemented with third-party support from a cyber security firm) to remediate the issue. As we talked, I briefed him at a high level on what happened, our current response activities, and what I needed in the way of resources to assist in the response. He approved the resources, thanked me for the call, and asked that I fly to meet him for a special gathering of the full board the following Wednesday to update them on the incident.

Proper incident response requires active involvement from the board, as well as informative and direct communication from the CISO. Briefings to the board on incident response should be reserved for large-scale attacks that involve adversarial occupation within the network, events that may cause large compliance or brand impact, or incidents involving significant disruption to the business. It can be easy for the board to be inundated with updates on broad-based incidents. Phishing attacks are rampant and usually it is the case that the security team can respond, triage, and remediate them quickly. Perhaps these types of attacks ought not be part of board involvement, but rather just updates during the regular briefings.

A general practice I have seen in my career is the management team and the board of directors come to an agreement on thresholds that would involve notifying the board of a cyber incident. In the notification policy, the thresholds for communicating are established, which members of the board are notified, which leaders from the management team notifies the board (and how), as well as expected timelines for notifying the selected members. This type of agreement, prior to an incident occurring, provides effective communications during the crisis.

SPECIAL PROJECTS

There may be occasions when the director reaches out to the CISO for assistance with special projects that span various tasks. As a trusted advisor to the board and one who deals with confidential matters daily, the CISO is a logical choice for supporting unique initiatives that often fall outside of normal CISO–board interactions. An example could include conducting investigations on behalf of the board that require the highest level of confidentiality. Leveraging the CISO for unique projects could provide the board with support options that may not have been immediately considered otherwise.

As you consider the various methods that you will leverage to engage your cyber security executive, a baseline component that is at the heart of understanding a corporation's security posture lies in an information security assessment. Chapter 5 highlights the assessment, as well as what to look for when reviewing your assessment results.

Note

1 A result that incorrectly identifies that a vulnerability exists.

Chapter 5

Information security assessment

An important part of any strategic journey is knowing where the organization is currently, and the best method for garnering this knowledge is through an initial assessment prior to developing a strategic plan. It provides a starting point by highlighting the current security posture for the organization and helps to do future prioritization of initiatives that will be forthcoming in the strategic plan.

As a director, you will not likely be part of performing the assessment; instead, you will be more focused on the results of the assessment. This chapter highlights the core components of a security assessment so that you can garner a better understanding of how the assessment was completed. This will position you to ask probing questions related to the results. The manner in which the results were generated is often as important as the final report itself.

A CISO can leverage many resources to help with assessing the security capabilities of a company. While not an exhaustive list, the following have proved helpful in my career, along with some tips for the director to inquire about the assessment processes used by their CISO.

CISO ASSESSMENT

You have spent the time to build the requirements for your CISO role, interviewed candidates, and invested time in beginning to build the relationship with your new security executive. Unless your qualification requirements for your CISO role were open to candidates who may have not previously served in such a role, your new CISO will have experience in assessing security programs. It is beneficial to leverage their years of experience as they will know what to look for, specifically the components that make for an effective security program. As they examine the effectiveness of the different security disciplines, they can weave in what they are learning about their new company. To supplement their lack of deep understanding of their new company at this point in their tenure, their interviews with

DOI: 10.1201/9781003477341-7

current employees are a great way to measure effectiveness of security controls.

Interview-based assessments begin with the CISO developing a list of very specific questions that target the different disciplines across information security. To supplement my expertise of cyber security, and to keep my series of questions industry-relevant and not created in a vacuum, I refer to common frameworks used in the security industry. Examples may include the National Institute of Standards and Technology 800 – 53 for Security and Privacy Controls for Information Systems and Organizations; (International Organization for Standardization (ISO)) 27000 key international standard for information security; and Center for Internet Security (CIS) Controls. These provide a foundation guide for effective security programs, and I reference them frequently, particularly during the assessment phase.

Meetings are scheduled with the internal information security team, employees from the IT organization, as well as representatives from the various lines of business and functional areas, including their leadership. While keeping the interviews conversational, I walk through my questions for a particular discipline, i.e., asset management, intrusion prevention, application security, and a host of others. I have found that to achieve the highest accuracy in the assessment, I will ask a question multiple times over the course of the assessment timeline and of different people, particularly if there is ambiguity in the initial response.

The current employees are a rich source of information for the assessment, after all, they have historical knowledge of the environment, but it is helpful to supplement the interview-based assessment with technical reviews as well. These will help validate the interview answers and give a more complete view into the security posture of the company. The CISO obtains access credentials to the multiple security platforms used by the security team and performs a review of how they are configured, recent alerts, and the overall health of the technology deployment. In addition to these technical checks, some third parties conduct technical assessments in the form of a compromise assessment, penetration testing, and other services. These reviews do not rely solely on human answers but instead review the technical aspects of the security program, which can prove extremely valuable for the initial assessment.

INTERNAL REPORTS

The new CISO can avail themselves to security assessments conducted by internal sources from the past few years to provide additional clarity to their initial assessment. Specific reports by the internal audit department and external auditor can provide valuable specifics on where gaps may exist in certain areas of the security program because they are more detailed than what external consultants may provide. However, these reports typically have a limited scope of review, i.e., data loss prevention program, the state of asset management, etc., and may not cover the entire security program. Regardless, they are a data point that can help to make the CISO assessment more comprehensive.

CONSULTANCY ASSESSMENTS

General security assessments from consultants can provide a quick review of the security program by leveraging common frameworks to deliver a maturity rating based on the common Capability Maturity Model Integration (CMMI) model. Often, the consultant may use an assessment model developed by their firm to provide more details into the risk posture for the client. There may be some of these models that are more marketing-driven instead of true risk measurements. An example may be measuring and scoring an adversary's ability (and desire) to break into the client's network. This type of adversarial information may be available for tightly organized hacking groups where attribution can be determined. However, as mentioned previously, some threat actors are not organized to a particular group or may work alone. Determining that lone person's hacking abilities and their specific desire to cause disruption to your specific corporate environment seems beyond the capabilities of a third-party consultancy. These types of assessments may not add value to the CISO assessment.

Third-party security program assessments are often primarily interview based and may only cover a short three-to-four-week service cycle. As a result, the findings are typically very broad in nature, after all, their view is that of an external one. The cost of these assessments should be considered as well, which could be very expensive for the client to just understand where the gaps lie, while not providing remediation to those gaps. Of course, the consultant group will promote their capabilities (at a separate cost) to assist the client in remediating those deficiencies.

In some cases, contractual or regulatory requirements may dictate that a security review be done by an external party. The most valuable type of consultant assessment will be those that employ deep technical testing services rather than general interview-based inquiries. Their results can be beneficial to both the management team and the CISO, providing each of them with technical, non-biased, and factual results that can be leveraged (in part) in building the strategic plan.

For you as a director, the bottom line for understanding the current risk posture for your company is to inquire the CISO how the assessment was performed, did it involve interview-based processes, technical reviews, or a combination of both? While it isn't necessary to grasp every component of the assessment, through an understanding of the methodology used in deriving the results, you will have a good understanding for how solid the results may be, and how likely the risk is of having to change direction mid-strategy.

Now that you are aware of the security posture for your organization; you'll want to understand how the CISO and management team will address the security program in an ongoing fashion. Chapter 6 highlights the prioritization, development, and communication process for the strategic security plan.

Chapter 6

The strategic plan

Building a cyber security strategic plan for a company requires close integration with the goals of the business and is dependent on a wide array of factors which make it nearly impossible to transfer one corporation's security strategy to another organization. Each company has a different risk profile, current security posture, and financial position that affects the timeline of the strategy.

While many management teams focus on three-year strategic plans, others may accelerate their cyber strategy due to specific risks to the company or perhaps critical gaps that cannot wait for progressive improvement. The availability of free operating cash flow to fund the security strategy is different from company to company which requires even more reliance on risk-based security investment decisions. Whatever timeline a company chooses to deploy their strategic plan, it is important for you to remember that the velocity of cyber risk moves very quickly, and three years can equate to a lifetime in the world of information security.

A good cyber strategy is one that prioritizes on risks to the company and doesn't try to quickly address every single need in the security domain. Your CISO should deliver a plan that takes the needs of the business (not just cyber security needs) and puts them into a realistic timeline that allows for efficient risk mitigation, not all at once, but not over the course of several years either. This is the point in time in which all the due diligence you've demonstrated in searching and selecting a CISO with strong business expertise (and at the same level as the other C-level executives of your team) pays dividends.

It was previously mentioned that a good briefing is done in such a way that facilitates easier decision-making for the management team. To accomplish this, cyber security strategies should have, at a minimum, three distinct categories: people, process, and technology. While they collectively are part of the larger cyber security strategy, each can be discussed individually with those executives of the management team responsible for those areas to gain their insights.

DOI: 10.1201/9781003477341-8

What follows is an in-depth view into each of the three categories mentioned previously, as they relate to building the cyber security strategy. Of course, each strategy will vary from CISO to CISO, but I have found that the tips I offer in each of the following sections have proven successful across the global corporations in which I was fortunate to have worked.

PEOPLE

Security vendors will sell their technology to anyone; they are not providing products and services to some CISOs and not to others. Each CISO is on a level playing field when it comes to security technology. Similarly, each CISO has access to best practices, research, and templates to deploy best of breed processes. Again, CISOs are on a level playing field in this area as well. *The true differentiator in a cyber security program lies in its people.* It is this category that separates the great security programs from the merely good ones.

Unfortunately, a quick scan of industry research will show that there are many cyber security jobs that go unfilled each year due to a shortage of available talent that possess these specialized skills. The number of unfilled jobs varies from report to report, but the bottom line is that our industry has more demand than resources to fulfill them. CISOs must take this barrier into account and imagine innovative ways to staff a security program and do so in a cost-effective way.

In the past few years, as the importance of cyber security grew even more and the talent gap widened, many people looked to the security industry as a logical choice for entering (or transitioning to) the field. As a hiring leader, a majority of the resumes that find their way to my inbox today are candidates with one, two, or three years of experience. In many cases, the resume has no security experience at all, but the candidate took a course to obtain a security certification in hopes of improving their hiring chances. Certification companies jumped at this market opportunity to provide "boot camps" and other fast certification prep courses to those who wish to accelerate their entrance into a hot industry. While these courses may provide theoretical foundations, they do not provide the hands-on type of experience that may be desired by companies to perform more advanced security roles.

The ability to fully staff a complete team of cyber professionals with five or more years of experience, preferably ten years, may not be feasible unless the company is willing to pay well over market for such talent. CISOs who promote strategies that include staffing the entire team with highly experienced security practitioners may not have realistic expectations for acquiring such a qualified team and as such, that strategy should be challenged.

I have found success in building teams by seeding the organization with just a few highly qualified candidates, and then filling the rest of the team with individuals who may not have significant cyber experience. In more than a few cases, I selected candidates with no security experience but had long tenures in the information technology field. The most critical attributes CISOs should look for in their non-security candidates are enthusiasm and curiosity. Individuals who demonstrate an energetic, highly enthusiastic manner are often the ones who reach out to others to consume the most knowledge they can on their new field. They typically volunteer to take on tasks so that they can acquire the knowledge to advance their career.

Another critical attribute for candidates is curiosity, the ability to question how things work. They look for the unintended uses of a technology and imagine how these unintended uses can be leveraged to bypass controls. These candidates will follow a potential issue all the way until it is fully understood. This is exactly the mindset that our adversaries have and to find candidates who possess this curiosity, but with an intent to do good, is extremely valuable.

Once I staff my team, I put them all together (in a room or virtually) so that they learn from one another. The experienced employees provide mentorship to the new teammates without cyber experience, and the new employees help to spark innovation by questioning the tenured teammates on the traditional ways of doing things. I have seen this strategy play out at multiple security programs I've led and the benefits of doing so have created productive, long-tenured security employees, nearly all of whom are still in the industry today and contributing greatly to our field.

Training for the cyber security staff is a critical element for the organization not only because it lends itself to retention of valuable resources but also assists in maintaining optimal operational capabilities of the security program. Training is important for all employees, but within cyber security, where risks evolve so rapidly, it is a necessity.

My goal is to attain a 70/20/10 rule when it comes to training. Seventy percent is actually doing the job, working with fellow teammates to complete the tasks at hand and learn from one another. Twenty percent is the training that an employee does on their own, perhaps reading books or looking online for opportunities to learn more about cyber security. The last ten percent is formal training, whether it is an industry conference or classroom instruction. While most employees tend to focus on the ten percent, I believe the remaining ninety percent is just as important to providing staff with security knowledge. Nevertheless, providing opportunities for security employees to attend conferences and interact with other members of the industry to share valuable information, and garner new relationships, should be a key component to the people aspect of any security strategy.

The CISO should place an annual budget placeholder in the strategic plan to address security training needs for the organization. Typically, I allot for enough funding to send everyone in the information security organization to at least one security conference per year, inclusive of travel to the event. It is a bulk amount for each employee to utilize how they wish, for whichever conference they choose, contingent on the fact that such training is related to the role that they hold in the security organization. If the employee serves on a conference committee, or perhaps speaks at a security conference, typically the conference will provide them with a free pass to the event. In doing so, the employee can then leverage their bucket of training dollars to attend more than one conference any given year. Lastly, when I procure (or renew) a security technology, I speak to the vendor during the negotiation process. I'll mention how I attended their annual conference and how valuable it was for me to learn more about their specific technology. They will agree by stating how proud they are of the annual event. Prior to executing the contract, I negotiate for ten free passes to their conference each year, every year, for the life of the contract. The combination of training dollars, employee involvement in the industry, and sponsorship by our vendors together provide nearly limitless opportunities for each security employee to learn, grow, and maintain effectiveness in a fast-paced industry.

As a director evaluating a security strategy, it is feasible for you to ask, "how many security employees should we have", or "how many is considered too many"? There is no magic formula to determine the appropriate amount of security personnel your company should employ. The number relies on several factors such as the risk posture for your company, the financial position of the company for adding new talent, and the current maturity of the information security program. However, in your review of the labor components to the security strategic plan, solid analysis should be demonstrated by the CISO on how the number was reached.

The first step the CISO performs is to identify the critical skill sets that are needed for the company's security program. These skills will provide the company with the requisite capabilities to perform the desired security services most important to its cyber journey that support business objectives. Next, the security executive assesses the skills of the current security team, then identifies gaps between desired and current states. A basic business school graphic can help outline the required competencies needed to fill the gaps (see Figure 6.1).

This simple exercise ensures that only the most critical needs are addressed first when building the people components of the cyber security program and reserving beneficial (but not critical) roles for onboarding later, as financial timing allows. Numerous influences impact the skills gap exercise and addressing them up front creates a well-rounded labor strategy that reduces the risk of irregular, perennial additions to the team. One such influence is highlighting single points of failure, the condition in which one person alone is responsible for a major security initiative or technology platform. Should that person go on vacation, call in sick, or perhaps leave the company, the

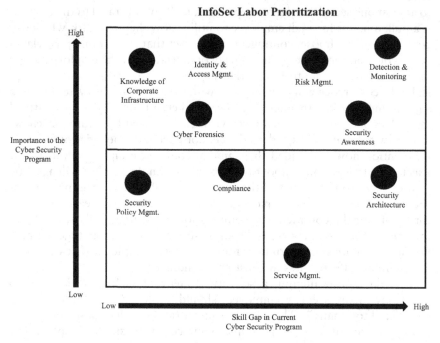

Figure 6.1 Labor prioritization.

security team is left struggling to catch up on the initiative which may cause service disruptions. Identifying these single points of failure and building a plan to remediate them should be an important part of the security labor strategy.

Demand management, the measurement of service requests (as well as anticipated future requests) from the lines of business and functional areas, will help the CISO to anticipate labor needs for their organization and build a strategy to ensure adequate service coverage. As a director, you are familiar with various forecasting tools available for business; leveraging similar forecasting methodologies, customized a bit for security, can be very beneficial in quantitatively measuring future service needs. Later in this book, we'll cover service management and some tips on using a security service management program to generate accurate data to describe demand needs.

Another influencer to building a security team is identifying and coordinating the blend of expertise that a CISO has on their team (as well as future expertise when hiring candidates). The team should have diverse experience that differs from person to person. Very much like a chess match, the CISO should strategize on the different competencies of each person and how they all fit together to provide a robust service capability. By having too many employees with experience in one domain and a lack of security professionals with knowledge in another discipline, the CISO may not have a good blend of expertise that optimizes a security program. Moreover, varying levels of expertise lend itself to enhanced collaboration among the team with an increased opportunity to share knowledge.

In the strategic plan, there should be a considerable amount of effort on standardizing job roles within the security organization. Of course, there will be highly specific job functions within areas of the team (vulnerability management, cyber security operations, etc.), but these roles could be bucketed into a job role called cyber security engineer, cyber security specialist, or something similar, with secondary titles addressing the distinctions within the job role. Job functions that relate to identity and access management (identity governance, privileged access management, etc.) can be bundled into an IAM Specialist or similar role. Standardizing security job roles accomplishes many things:

1. *Right Compensation for the Right Role:* Not all security functions require the same technical level of cyber fluency. As a result, not all compensation models are the same for cyber professionals with these varying levels of fluency. Persons who hold roles that focus on compliance or security policy management, for instance, may not need the same level of technical skill as that of a cyber security engineer or specialist. To ensure the appropriate amount of compensation is applied, clear distinctions should be made through job standardization to avoid lumping all security domains together just because they are in the cyber industry. Having said that, some seemingly less than technical roles, such as a security awareness and training specialist, do indeed require significant knowledge in information security. Without it, if an awareness specialist is tasked with writing an awareness article on multi-factor authentication and they don't understand the topic, they may need to go to a cyber security engineer to fill in their gaps of knowledge. In doing so, the company is now paying two people to perform the work of writing the article that should be done by one employee.

2. *Job Role Leveling:* To retain excellent talent, fair and competitive salaries must be paid to your information security professionals. To accomplish this, human resources (or a third party engaged by human resources) performs industry comparisons to what the company is paying against compensation data from other companies in similar regions, industries, and job role types. To get the most accurate benchmark for industry pay bands, standardizing job roles to the functions the employee performs helps in the compensation analysis process by aligning job roles to ones that are common in the industry. In my career, it was not uncommon for me to discover in

my initial assessment of a company a larger than normal amount of cyber security architects. As I dug deeper, I realized that nearly all the security architects were not performing the role of security architect, instead, they were typically executing the duties of a cyber security engineer. Misalignment to a job role, such as the architect, may occur for different reasons but one that comes to mind is the industry compensation band for a security architect is usually much higher than that of a security operations employee. Whatever the reason, standardizing job roles helps to pay security employees an appropriate salary while saving the company money in mis-aligned labor costs.

3. *The Distinction of Leadership:* There may a belief among security professionals (or in any discipline for that matter) that when an employee works their way up in a company by performing well in individual contributor roles, the next logical step is moving into leadership. Perhaps such a promotion would include a managerial role in one of security domains, or a director role leading several functions within cyber security. I have consistently counseled employees to make the decision to move into management only after significant reflection because once the move to leadership occurs, the individual will find the role to be completely different from that of an individual contributor. Leaders trade the excitement of working with security platforms, for budget spreadsheets and performance management discussions. When creating and standardizing job roles, the CISO must ensure that leadership roles are aligned to the primary function: *supporting the employees under their leadership.* If a leader is configuring cyber security systems, they are not focused on providing constant support and operational oversight to their employees, and they are robbing the security employees on their team of the opportunity to learn and grow. Additionally, companies end up paying leaders higher salaries for job functions that should be done by the individual contributors on the team.

4. *Career Path Clarity:* When I arrived at one of the companies I worked for in the past, I found forty-one distinct job roles within the cyber security organization, for a team with just forty-three employees in total. With so many specialized job titles, it is difficult for employees, particularly new members to the team, to understand career progression. Job standardization aids in providing clarity on how the roles are leveled, as well as how they progress in responsibilities, so that the employees can better plan their career development.

A company relies on third-party assistance in performing cyber security services, therefore the people aspect of the strategic plan should detail which services will be conducted in house, and which will be outsourced. Many potential benefits, as well as limitations, exist that lead to the decision on whether or not to outsource a specific security service (more on this later).

Newer types of security roles have emerged within companies in (somewhat) recent years that provide unique services to the information security program. Roles such as deputy CISO, security chief of staff, security coordination specialist, and many other unique titles are increasingly finding their way into labor requests. You should explore the details of these job functions, what tangible value they provide, and what is the driver for the creation of the dedicated role. In some cases, perhaps in enormous global corporations, it may make sense to have such roles to satisfy the overwhelming service demand from the various lines of business and operating segments. In other corporations however, the role may be duplicative to other functions with no clear cost benefit.

For example, a chief of staff role may include duties such as strategic planning, project management, analytics, or perhaps communication – all focused on the information security program. It could be argued that there are other enterprise roles (or maybe roles within the security department) that could be leveraged to perform such functions in a medium to large corporations, rather than hiring a dedicated security resource.

Regarding the deputy CISO role, a justification may include preparing another person to take on the primary CISO role, should the current CISO leave the company. You may find that staffing a specific deputy CISO role solely for this purpose may not make good financial sense. Identifying high-performing leaders inside the current security organization, developing their skills, providing them with security projects that stretch them, and affording them the opportunity to present to senior leadership will address the concern of "bench strength", without the cost of a dedicated resource. Moreover, a named deputy CISO eliminates the hope of opportunity for other high-performing leaders in the security organization to view themselves as a potential successor. Yet, there may be other circumstances that validate the need for this role, so it is the responsibility of the CISO to make a strong business case for justifying the cost of this added resource for that need.

In mid- to large-sized corporations, it may be beneficial for the CISO to create a role that facilitates service delivery in a proactive fashion. Roles such as business information security officer (BISO), cyber risk partner, security business analyst, or a multitude of other titles, serve as the conduit between the lines of business and the core cyber security organization. There may be a few of these roles within the security organization, each one assigned to a particular business segment, functional area, international region, or a host of other alignment options.

The role sits with the assigned business areas, attends their recurring meetings, builds relationships across the segment, and garners an important understanding of the upcoming plans and strategies for that area of the business. They take this knowledge back to the appropriate service tower within the core information security team, who in turn executes and delivers the actual service. In doing so, the security team is made aware of initiatives in advance, which facilitates lower costs to projects and a reduced risk of time delays to the business. I have found success in assigning these roles for a period of eighteen months, then rotating the individuals in the role to another segment so that at the end of the rotation cycle, each one has a 360-degree view of the company. Adding such a role could provide value if it fits within the needs and structure of the company. For very small companies, such a role may not be needed as the duties could potentially be consumed by the current staff.

The professionals that make up your security program will ultimately determine the success of your program. Stringent analysis and strategic forethought by the CISO, with detail-oriented questioning of the strategy by management and yourself, help to ensure that the people category is complete and without cost prohibitive redundancies.

PROCESS

Prior to enhancing existing security processes, or creating new ones, it is critical that the CISO has a strong knowledge of the business and how security fits within it. Nearly every security process within a cyber program is only effective if it is customized to the rhythm of the business, or operational cadence of the corporation. The best way to garner this business insight is to regularly tour the corporate offices and facilities to talk with employees. A great CISO is rarely in their office. I argue that those security executives who sit behind their desk for eight hours a day, behind an impressive bank of four to five computer monitors, are not working to make their role as successful as it could be.

In the Fall of 2002, I was touring one of the manufacturing plants of the company where I was the CISO. It was fascinating to watch how raw materials were transformed into high-quality products that our customers loved, and to watch the skill (and pride) of the employees in creating value. I spoke with employees and learned more about each of their duties. I learned about the systems and machinery that were used, as well as the processes for ensuring all shifts had accurate work orders to meet fluctuating demand.

Fast forward two months, one of the employees from our Security Operations Center approached me on a Thursday and said there was a critical patch to address a vulnerability was released, but one of the manufacturing plants was pushing back on patching the system due to work schedules. I realized it was one of the plants that I previously visited and told the security employee that this plant operated more than one shift with an hour between each shift. That hour was used to set up order tickets and stage materials for production by the next shift. I also learned that each

Saturday morning they had a maintenance window of a few hours when they did preventative maintenance on equipment. I asked the employee why can't we inquire about patching the system during this maintenance time, so we don't impact production? As a result, the security of the system was addressed, and production was not impacted. Without this local knowledge of the business, uninformed decisions could perpetuate the longstanding myth that cyber security is an impediment to the business rather than what it truly can be: an enabler and protector of the business.

While it is critical to take the needs of the business into account when enhancing processes, these initiatives cannot be done in a vacuum that is insulated from the outside world. Strategies and processes should also have an industry view to make them optimally effective and externally relevant. A good method for accomplishing this is with the use of the security frameworks that were previously mentioned. They can serve as an effective guide to establishing process controls by detailing several common domains of cyber security, as well as the specific controls (at varying levels).

Frequently, companies will leverage industry research firms to garner more information on best practices to implement effective processes. Through research data, one-on-one discussions with analysts, or the use of peer security member forums, the CISO can compare their process improvement plans to other programs to better understand potential gaps in coverage.

One of the best methods for attaining an external perspective is for the CISO to leverage their network of peers. On many occasions I have reached out to peer CISOs to learn insightful tips on a particular process, how they implemented it, lessons learned, as well as pitfalls to avoid. Since all security programs are vastly different from one another, this feedback serves merely as an insightful data point, something that usually requires some customization to fit the needs of my company's security program. What is interesting is that the cyber industry is a tight, collaborative group and when garnering insights from peers, even from competitors to your company, all competition is stripped away for the shared mission of stopping adversaries.

Many hackers are lazy, those that are not simply don't want to unreasonably over-invest time and resources to break into a network unless that time is necessary to meet their objective. For many adversaries, they have an arsenal of techniques and malware at their disposal. In some cases, threat actors will build custom malware specific to a particular engagement. However, they don't want to use their best weapons until they must. Instead, they look for the open doors and windows of a corporate network, perhaps an unpatched system with a vulnerability, or maybe sending a phishing email to an unsuspecting employee. Whatever the path of least resistance, they will use that vector to accomplish their mission.

So, when it comes to building processes for your information security program, the CISO should start with the fundamentals first. It may be attractive to create next-generation security capabilities, but to do so without tending to the foundational items first, significant cost may be added to the program that leaves residual risk to the simple basics. The CISO's strategy for developing security processes should begin with foundational things that address vulnerabilities, security awareness, security policy management, and risk management, to name a few. Once these are matured to an acceptable level, then more advanced processes can be added to the portfolio of security services.

INFORMATION SECURITY GOVERNANCE

It is important for employees to understand that the CISO and their team do not arbitrarily make up security policies based on individual beliefs on risks. The expectations for each employee as it relates to information security are done through security policies. These policy decisions should come from executive leadership based on the corporate stance for a particular security topic, i.e., using personal computing devices for corporate work, etc.

One method to create these high-level policies is through an Information Security Governance Committee, or perhaps called the Information Security Steering Committee. Usually chaired by the CISO and formally chartered, the committee membership may include, the CEO, CFO, CIO, General Counsel, Leader of Internal Audit, and CHRO, at a minimum. The committee meets quarterly to discuss information security topics, allocate security resources to security initiatives, arbitrate conflicts for security support to competing business initiatives, establish policy requirements, and garner bi-directional feedback on the performance of the cyber security program.

The last thing any group desires is another committee, but the importance of the Information Security Committee is critical to the protection of the corporation, and at a cost of only an hour each quarter. Things can be done to enhance the productivity of the committee meetings. For starters, it should be set up so that eighty percent of the work is completed outside of the actual committee meeting. If each meeting consists solely of the CISO presenting slides for the attendees to listen to and ask an occasional question, the longevity of the meeting will suffer. Instead, when this impressive roster of executives assembles, the meetings should be conversational to a well-planned agenda with the goal of making them decision based in nature. Every major leadership representative of the corporation is in a room (or virtual), why pass up an extraordinary opportunity to make the committee optimally effective?

Preparation is key. Building a collaboration space in your company's standard technology platform helps to organize all the information. A calendar of committee meetings and events, committee member pre-reading materials, the agenda, and an area for supplemental reading or industry reports will all prove valuable. If timed well, the outputs from the Information Security Committee can be used to seed the topics for the upcoming board of directors information security update.

When developing the agenda, it is wise for the CISO to obtain feedback from the committee members on what topics may be of interest to them. Supplemented with CISO-driven topics, the agenda will serve the departmental concerns of each participant. Once developed, the agenda is posted with each topical area outlined, who leads the discussion, links to any pre-readings, and an icon that highlights if the agenda item is informational only, an open discussion, or if a decision is needed. By highlighting the expectations for each agenda topic up front, each committee person understands desired outcomes and can better prepare for the meeting.

Pre-reading materials are crucial to an effective committee flow. I've never met an executive who doesn't like to see materials prior to a discussion, and when it comes to the Information Security Committee, it is essential. Such material highlights any concerns, associated metrics or reports that detail the issue, options for remediation, and recommendations by the CISO on a proposed path forward. For example, if an agenda item relies on an informative discussion (or decision) involving multiple references to a particular framework, perhaps NIST, it may be valuable to include the NIST framework (or applicable portions of it) in the supplemental reading so each committee person can familiarize themselves with it.

All these committee materials are uploaded to the collaboration platform at least one to two weeks in advance of the meeting to give each member the opportunity to read, research, form questions, as well as opinions on the path forward for each agenda item. In doing so, the meeting will be more productive, and you will have realized the importance of one of the key tenets in an effective CISO's competencies: communicating in such a way to make the decision-making process easier for the audience. Lastly, it may prove beneficial to have a member of the CISO's team, perhaps a high-performing leader, attend the meeting to give them exposure to the executive team and serve as a scribe to take notes and minutes from the meeting. Rotating multiple, high-performing employees into this administrative role could aid in creating the bench strength previously mentioned in this book.

CENTRALIZATION VS. DE-CENTRALIZATION

It is common in many corporations to have a centralized cyber security function with global reach that provides services to all entities within the company. Shared service, center of excellence, enterprise security, or whatever the organization may be called, this centralized model provides many benefits. In other corporations, a de-centralized model is chosen with two or more groups providing cyber security services to different portions of the corporation. This model can be effective for some organizations, as well. So, which is the right model for your company? Because security programs are so unique, the answer lies in how the model aids in the delivery of security services for your particular corporation to lower risk, and in the most cost-effective way.

In the mid-2000s, I led the security program for one of the operating sectors of an enormous global corporation. My sector alone had a revenue stream of approximately $5 billion with 35,000 employees, and the company had nine of these operating sectors at the time, each with their own information security executive. They sat with the local sector leadership and provided customized support to their security needs, while reporting to the corporate vice president and CISO for the corporation. Aside from a centralized security operations center that provided technical services to the entire company, each sector had their own cyber security program with a dedicated local security staff.

In addition to the internal cyber security teams, there was a separate cyber security division that provided security services to external customers. All these separate programs converged annually (at a minimum) for a series of offsite meetings to share sector security information and best practices. Each entity had their own risk profile, unique regulations that it needed to comply with, and varying business goals to achieve. This is a good example of a de-centralized security model that best fit the needs of the company at that time.

Two years into my role as a security executive for the sector at this company, I was awarded the newly created position of enterprise information security officer. My new role was responsible for taking nine disparate security organizations and striving for a holistic security program, all while maintaining the de-centralized model. This format worked well for the company at the time, providing local support while federating similar capabilities to address risk.

As the CISO for a few other mid- to large-sized companies, there were traces of separate information security teams, in addition to the centralized organization which served the majority of the company. These disparate teams sprung up usually as a result of an acquisition of a company, or perhaps the desire for regional or dedicated security support to a particular business segment by that leader. In de-centralized cases such as these, the value of separate teams may not be as high, simply because there may be no clear business driver for doing so. It introduces gaps in security maturity across the teams and lends itself to a hyper focus on addressing security initiatives for a particular segment over another.

When I arrived as the new CISO for a mid-sized corporation, I was speaking with one of the security managers who reported to me on the enterprise team; he was the product of an acquisition. As a result, his focus was on the security of that (now) business unit of the company. I asked him what type of perimeter security products we used at the company and when he told me, I commented that the specific product was a very good one. He agreed and added, "Now, I don't know what they use in the other business units, but that is what we use here in my business unit". I had my work cut out for me.

Disparate security focus within a corporation could potentially introduce significant risk, and disproportionate levels of security expertise among the different teams could cause unnecessary maturity variances in the security posture of the company. In the deteriorated perimeter environment in which many companies operate, small vulnerabilities in one segment could introduce risk for the entire corporation. For example, when going on vacation, it is prudent for homeowners to double check the locks on their windows and doors prior to leaving for their destination. If everything is locked up tight, except for one small window in the rear of the house, the solid security of the rest of the home doesn't matter. A burglar will use any opening they can find to gain unlawful entry. Similarly, if there are robust controls in place across the corporate network, but just one small, non-critical system in another segment (under another security team's jurisdiction) has significant vulnerabilities, an intruder will target that system to gain entry and attempt lateral movement to other, more critical systems. Additionally, de-centralized security functions could potentially lead to confusion in roles, responsibilities, and disproportionate security controls in corporate networks.

It could be argued that certain networks in a de-centralized security service model could be segmented from the other areas of the technology landscape. While segmentation is a very good practice in general, without clear business requirements to justify the segmentation of security programs, as well as the overhead operating costs of creating and maintaining such a model across multiple security teams, may prove too costly. De-centralization introduces another finance-related complexity, as well. It will become increasingly difficult for a CISO to answer a basic question from the CFO or CEO: "How much do we spend on cyber security at our corporation each year"?

Centralization of the security program on the other hand can be a cost-effective, value-added structure for most companies. It organizes security in a central center of excellence that provides security services to the entire corporation. In doing so, a company only needs to build the capabilities within one organization to avoid duplicative technology spend (and opens up enterprise discounts from vendors for larger purchases instead of several smaller ones); it centralizes security processes and maintains one team of experts following the same security vision for the company (see Figure 6.2).

Pursuing a centralized security program is maximally efficient when an Information Security Charter (policy document) is created and executed by

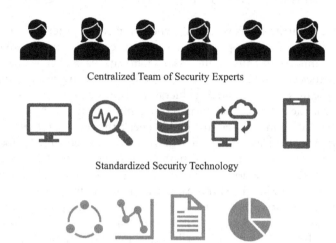

Centralized Security Model

Centralized Team of Security Experts

Standardized Security Technology

Common Enterprise Security Processes

Figure 6.2 Centralized security model.

the CEO of the company. The Charter dictates that information security is critically important to the company, that security is every employee's responsibility to help protect corporate resources, and the CISO (without specific names) and their organization are responsible for the creation and operational oversight of the company's information security program. This simple document outlines clear responsibilities for all stakeholders and enforces the centralization of the security program.

Following a centralized model does not mean that regional considerations cannot be met. It is valuable for a global corporation to sprinkle security resources across multiple geographic regions to provide close touch service to local support needs. Achieving a balance between this regional support and federation of an enterprise program is not easy; local resources may lean more heavily on the geographic area in which they sit. However, if done correctly, the enterprise program can enjoy a global style of support, and employees across the globe can gain experience in working on multiple different initiatives outside of their country.

The choice between a centralized and de-centralized model should be made after significant analysis of the speed and cost of security services provided to the corporation is measured. Once a decision has been made, whichever it may be, organizations should maintain this model and squelch the sporadic building of additional cyber security teams.

TECHNOLOGY

It is no exaggeration to say that the cyber security technology market has exploded in recent years. At security conferences each year, organizers are adding more and more technology showroom floor space to accommodate the influx of new cyber companies. CISOs are bombarded with cold calls on office phones, mobile phones, email, text messages, social media, and informational mailings, to introduce new (proposed) best of breed capabilities that could displace other security tools and provide the CISO with a more accurate view of threats in a "single pane of glass".

Today's security product industry is heavily focused on a marketing-driven strategy that often claims to solve nearly all the security woes for a company. Unlike other industries where customers dictate the demand and the natural market evolution follows (i.e., the elimination of certain styles/models of vehicles due to a lack in demand), cyber security companies often look to dictate the security demands for the consumer, telling the customer what they should be concerned with, along with a special product that addresses all those demands. As CISOs continue to do more in clearly conveying their needs to reduce risk, this trend will reverse itself to better align with a consumer-driven demand cycle. Until this is realized, our cyber industry will always have security vendors offering up products that seemingly provide a quick fix to a problem that doesn't have a quick fix.

Yet vendors in the cyber security space are very much needed and many provide exceptional products and services. Together as partners, security teams and vendors work to stifle the onslaught of breaches. It is up to the CISO to evaluate capabilities and find those vendors who seek to be the best in their field with a significant focus on quality of service.

Acquisitions are rampant in the cyber market with companies acquiring startups and other corporations to expand their security portfolio. Previous niche players have been woven into large cyber security juggernauts that can provide an offering to a multitude of security needs. Often these vendors look to consolidate all security products for a customer into one platform, eliminating a consumer's need for multiple security suppliers. You should look for strategies within the technology section of the CISO strategic plan that discuss the blending of vendors, versus an all-in-one security provider, to determine how the choice was made.

Like so many other areas of the strategic plan (and quickly becoming a main theme for this book), there is no one strategy that fits all corporations. However, thoughtful research into the risks and financial aspects of each technology strategy should be demonstrated in the plan. Having many unique products often provides very good capabilities because each vendor focuses on one thing and, as a result, may do it better than their competitors. Leveraging multiple security vendors though may introduce more complexity when weaving the different solutions together, ensuring that they complement one another, and avoiding negative interoperability issues. But by consolidating security technologies to one vendor, it may raise the risk of "having all your eggs in one basket" which could cause disruption if a significant flaw or vulnerability is discovered in that vendor's platform.

Increasingly present are vendor models that bundle general IT office technologies along with technologies in other industry verticals such as collaboration tools, cyber security, audio/video capabilities, and many more. The consumer pays one price which bundles all these solutions into one enterprise license. The dialogue between the vendor and the CIO then transitions to "why would you pay for all these separate security vendors when you get it for free with the license cost you are already paying with our product"? It is a compelling question and one that the CIO immediately asks of the CISO. While many companies successfully leverage vendors with this model and the interoperability enjoyed by having varying capabilities in one solution, there are three potential concerns; let's outline those concerns next.

As just mentioned, having all cyber security technologies with one provider could surface issues if there is an outage or vulnerability with the vendor. Next, not all technologies are "free" with the license cost. Advanced capabilities within a technology may come at an additional cost, which dilutes the value by increasingly higher add-on costs. Lastly, as threats evolve, it is increasingly difficult for vendors to be experts across all technology domains.

For sports fans, you may have noticed the infrequent trend of an exceptional talent in one professional sport attempting to break into another. Perhaps a professional basketball player attempting a career in baseball, or maybe an all-star football player trying the same transition to multiple, other sports. Rarely do we see examples where that athlete has achieved mastery in all fields, and on all fields.

As another example, many diners enjoy an evening meal at a restaurant that specializes in a specific type of food, perhaps Cajun cuisine, or maybe Italian fare. The food, for the most part, is focused on one style and they build their establishment around it, with diners enjoying the unique style, flavors, and ambiance it has to offer. Rarely have I gone into a restaurant and found exceptional meals by an establishment that serves up a multitude of various options including jambalaya, pasta primavera, Asian fried rice, pizza, barbeque, enchiladas, sushi, hamburgers, and Thai options, all on one menu. Trying to master everything (in any field) does indeed lead to a larger scope of capabilities but may lead to reduced expertise in each of those capabilities.

The bottom line for a security technology strategy ultimately comes down to a simple mantra. *The CISO should allow the strategy to drive technology choices and not allow technology to drive the strategy.* I have never sat in a vendor briefing of their technology and thought to myself, "wow, I didn't know that was a risk I should have been thinking about".

Once the roster of security technologies has been identified, the strategic plan should include language on how the technologies will be implemented, and on what timeline based on prioritization. As a director, you need not be involved in managing the details of the implementation strategy; however, it is important for you to understand the broad themes of implementation to ensure it is included in the CISO thought process in building the technology portfolio. As more and more technologies are approved for purchase, the more difficult the implementation cycle, especially if there are limited security resources for the company.

It would seem logical to include professional services in the purchase to help quick start implementation, but there are some areas to watch out for when leveraging these services. The vendor wants the implementation to go well so that the value of the product is fully realized. CISOs need a successful implementation as well to ensure optimal value of the purchase. The *manner* in which the execution of the services is achieved requires forethought.

Like all other service providers, vendors have a team of implementation specialists that have competing engagements so it may not be realistic to plan for an immediate professional services engagement by the vendor. There may be a backlog of implementations that push your professional services out for several weeks, and this delay needs to be considered, especially when implementing more than one product or service from multiple vendors. Appropriate scheduling with the various vendors ensures that those with shorter backlogs may perform professional services first, and other partners with longer backlogs can assist later in the strategy.

Next, solid preparation prior to the vendor's implementation team arriving includes ensuring the CISO's team, and other departmental resources are ready for the engagement. Having the appropriate resources ready to go when the vendor arrives helps to reduce the risk of the vendor's professional services team sitting around waiting (at a cost to your company) while internal resources are preparing.

Lastly, the professional services should be a partnership during the implementation. The service should be to assist the internal team with standing up a product and not solely doing all of it on behalf of your company. It becomes problematic to have professional services implement a product on their own and when they leave, the internal team knows very little about the implementation, its configuration, and ongoing operation. When future new configuration needs arise, the customer will require further support by the vendor, and it may be the case that the vendor will charge for those new services. By having the internal team learn and become familiar with the technology deployment during the professional services engagement, this costly risk can be avoided.

CLOUD VS. ON-PREMISES

A key decision to any security strategy's technology plan often lies on the choice to host those cyber security technologies on premises in your own data centers or leveraging a cloud infrastructure managed by a third party. The movement to the cloud may provide security benefits by leveraging the best of breed computing resources, as a service, from a variety of different companies, i.e., Amazon Web Services, (AWS) Microsoft, (Azure), Google, etc. These cloud vendors absorb the capital expenditures needed to provide computing infrastructures and often include security-specific offerings (at an additional cost) to help further protect the customer's computing instance. But leveraging the cloud does not equate to dropping in your company's infrastructure with the expectation that the vendor will be responsible for the security of your environment. Cloud providers are very clear about responsibilities in their cloud service, and they document those responsibilities for their customers to understand. They will be responsible for the compute, storage, networking software, and infrastructure-related services. The customer is responsible for the security of the customer data, platform, applications, network and firewall configurations, encryption, and the access components of the service.

More and more vendors of security products are providing cloud options for their customers, some security vendors even choosing a cloud-only type of deployment, where the product is hosted exclusively in the cloud without any options to have an on-premises version.

The benefits of a cloud-first strategy may include transitioning much of the procurement, configuration, and oversight of on-premises hardware and software to the vendor, which frees up internal resources to focus on core competencies in cyber security. As with any solution, there are risks associated with cloud computing (more on these later). Directors should be fully aware of the cloud vs. on-premises decision and how that decision was factored into the strategic planning for the security organization at their company.

PUBLISHING THE STRATEGY

The CISOs, in partnership with the information security organization, leadership, and other company departments, have finalized the strategic plan for security and are ready to share it broadly across the corporation. Gaining approval for the strategy is the first priority and as such, leadership should be the initial audience who sees the final strategic plan.

Previously I suggested some tips in making the decision process easier by setting up one-on-one meetings with the CIO, CHRO, CFO, general counsel, etc. to show them the strategy components that may be of the most interest to each of them. Once their support and feedback are obtained, the

CISO should present to the CEO and his or her direct reports to get final approval on the plan. This approval accomplishes a few things, not the least of which allocates financial and labor resources (if required) to accomplish the strategy. Next, it shows top leadership support for the importance of executing the cyber security strategy to the employees of the corporation.

The board of directors, through a committee or the full board, can then briefed on the top risks for the company and the strategy to address them. Using the tips within this book, directors can inquire about specific points within the strategy to better understand the building blocks for the strategic plan, agree with the direction of the program, and advise on matters related to cyber security.

Armed with the approvals and alignment from senior leadership and the board, the CISO is ready to begin the work of promoting the strategic plan with the rest of the company. All too often, security strategies are well known to the information security organization but remain a mystery outside this team. CISOs should not perpetuate a common stereotype that security is done behind the scenes in secrecy, far away from the business. In reality, security is part of the business, an enabler to those functions with direct impact to top-line revenue growth and/or bottom-line efficiencies. Isn't it appropriate then that the cyber security strategy should be widely marketed across the business? Through corporate town halls, sales kick-off sessions, IT team meetings, or whatever the venue, capturing each opportunity to discuss the strategic vision of the security program helps to solicit wide-ranging support.

Extremely important is the notion of tailoring these presentations to the audience by customizing each one. There are baseline portions of the plan to communicate to everyone, but the best marketing of the strategy comes with explaining how the strategy effects the specific job roles of the listening audience. What can they expect? How can they assist with the security vision? By tailoring the presentations to the audience, participants will be more actively engaged and feel more comfortable with asking insightful questions.

There has been a tremendous amount of work that went into assessing the security posture of the company and creating a strategy to optimally address risk for your company. It was accomplished through hard work by multiple teams over several months to get to this milestone. And after all this effort should come the realization that your CISO has led your company not to the finish line; no, the work is just starting. Execution to the strategic plan has numerous important layers, and we'll look into those in Chapter 7.

Chapter 7

The importance of execution

It would be difficult to find an executive at any large corporation who doesn't believe that cyber security is an important topic that should be addressed. Within the end user population of a corporation, the overwhelming majority of them seek to do the right thing when it comes to protecting information and will follow cyber policies. I have found throughout my career that the area which holds the most debate and conflict in implementing security strategies lies at the manager and director levels. These are the levels where ideas become reality and where operational collisions may take place most often. These are the leaders who manage aggressive project schedules, with limited labor resources and dwindling budgets. In short, this is the level where execution happens.

When most people hear of conflict, they may think of a negative connotation, usually imagining an argument between two or more people. I suggest that conflict is actually a good thing, and if done professionally can enhance the implementation of projects. It is through conflict where innovations are surfaced – a positive byproduct of effective teamwork. Yet, we often find ourselves avoiding conflict or in many cases give up on trying to come to a solution that meets security needs while not interfering too much with business goals.

To help illustrate this point, there is a common document that has been swirling through the security industry for years called a risk acceptance form. While they differ in content, format, and the execution of the form, its basic function is to transfer risk. For example, security may be working with a small regional IT team to implement a security control that will help protect the overall company. The rest of the global IT teams adhered to the control and implemented it effectively. But this particular regional IT team pushes back explaining that they understand the goal of the security control, but it would negatively impact their business and would prefer if they did not have to implement the security initiative. The security team then explains why the control is so important and that it is part of a larger project to do this globally at the corporation. The small IT group reiterates that

DOI: 10.1201/9781003477341-9

they understand the need for it, but they just can't impact the business and prefer not to implement the control. After considerable back and forth, the discussion concludes with the security executive providing a form to a leader within the regional team (director, VP, or higher level is best) that explains the needed security control and that the team under the leader's supervision does not want to implement the control. It may also describe the risks associated with not implementing it, as well as a full understanding that if the risk is realized, the leader of that regional team takes full responsibility for any negative outcome or impact. The leader signs the form, and the security team files it away in case it is needed in the future to demonstrate unsuccessful attempts at mitigating the risk to this portion of the business.

I've always disliked these forms.

To me, it is a white flag of surrender in which the security leader says, "I've tried to work with this team, we cannot come to an agreement, therefore we are giving up and having them accept all the risk of not doing it".

Aside from my personal opinions on the matter, there are very real problems with leveraging such a form. It was mentioned previously that the network perimeter has significantly eroded and that a vulnerability in one small area can lead to adversarial exploitation with subsequent lateral movement to other critical areas of the network. By signing the risk acceptance form, the leader of that small regional team is not just accepting the risk for his or her area but may be accepting risk for the entire corporation – something they may not have the authority to accept.

Examples such as these help to demonstrate the struggle of executing a security strategy; ask any CISO and they will provide clear memories of project struggles throughout their career. While there is no one size fits all cure to execution conflict (and I would suggest there should not be a desire for one), there are tips that can help to lessen the impact of conflict and better align stakeholders to the goals of security strategy.

CLEAR DIRECTION

Prior to execution planning, the CISO has hopefully shared the security strategy with a wide audience of employees and leaders. The CISO has shown not only all the elements of the plan that was approved by leadership but how the plan fits to what each team receiving the presentation does in their organizations. Even better, the CISO would have incorporated feedback, concerns, and ideas that were learned in building the strategy to anticipate potential issues during execution, and plan as much as possible for those issues in advance. Sharing details of the strategy across a wide audience helps to align the direction of where the company is going with information security as well as the expectations for employees in the pursuit of cyber fluency across the enterprise.

PLANNING AND FOLLOW-THROUGH

Outlining clear milestones and tasks, then measuring progress to them, is critical for execution. Ask ten people and you will get ten different preferences for tools that can effectively track progress to project tasks and milestones. The key for your cyber security program is to choose one of them and ensure all stakeholders are leveraging the same solution. Also important is to confirm that the platform used is a corporate standard to provide adequate security controls to protect the information, as well as reduce the cost of multiple project planning tools. Once the underpinnings of tracking progress have been established, the CISO can then begin to inspect progress to the execution goals. The objective is to ensure that steady progress is made, even if only a limited number of minutes each week, establishing a mindset that continual advancement toward completion is critical.

REGULAR REVIEWS

Documenting tasks, accountable parties, percentage complete, and project timelines are important for confirming that projects are understood by all stakeholders. Measuring the completion of tasks through actionable metrics paves the way for success, as well. However, documents and graphs are useless if the data is not reviewed on a regular basis. Through recurring project review meetings, security leaders can discuss progress (or lack thereof) to initiatives and assist the team with removing any barriers to progress.

Traversing through each project regularly provides the team with the opportunity to discuss completion to tasks, as well as highlight items that should be included in the plan that may have been left out from the original project. It is a chance to reallocate resources from projects that are ahead of schedule to those that may be behind or require more assistance. These reviews are a wonderful way to seed updates on the execution of the strategy for senior leaders of the company when the CISO presents to them. Ultimately, without regular meetings to review progress, the execution of the strategy may be hindered, even though a substantial amount of documentation exists.

You need not be involved in the execution details of the strategic plan; the aforementioned tips, however, may prove insightful if you find that the strategy's timing is consistently offtrack. Questioning and understanding the execution methodology being used may provide insights into why the schedule is not being met.

Chapter 8

Financing cyber security

I don't overly worry if I will obtain security funding. My concerns are more geared to how I obtain the funding so as not to exert unnecessary fiscal pressure on the company.

In the end, CISOs will ultimately receive the budget that is needed to enhance a cyber security program. It is not a case of *if* a company will provide security funding, but *how* they will provide that funding. Will it be funded incrementally over time, based on prioritized risk, and through a thoughtful budget cycle year over year? Or will it be funded all at once in the wake of a massive cyber breach when chaos has ensued, with business partners and auditors asking questions about the security of the company and what is being done to reduce the risk of future events?

We should not put complete and total reliance in cyber insurance to calm ourselves of the financial impacts related to a breach. Policies typically only cover response-type expenses associated with the event and not costs for preventative types of purchases to increase the post-breach security posture of the company, which can be significant.

The role of the CISO is to provide guidance to leadership on the security posture of the company, its vulnerabilities, realistic threats (and likelihood) to those vulnerabilities, potential remediations, and a proposed plan to fund those remediations over time with a budget strategy. At this point, your due diligence in searching for a CISO candidate with strong financial knowledge, as well as a broader fiscal consciousness to non-security needs, will be beneficial. The CISO is tasked with outlining all of the requisite information for leadership with the goal of minimizing the financial impacts to the company both before and after a potential breach. Options are then presented to reduce risk through budget additions to the security program for executives to consider. It is then the decision of the executive team on how to fund the security program based on the CISO's budget proposal.

How much should a company invest in cyber security? With so many variables in play, benchmarking security funding is a tricky endeavor that often does not lead to clear guidance on the appropriate amount to budget for a company. If a corporation leverages a de-centralized security model with multiple teams performing security services, understanding the total security spend may prove even more difficult. Even with all the security capabilities assembled into one organization with the total spend understood in great detail, the notion of comparing that spend to other security programs across similar industries, company size, etc., may not yield the desired results that provide actionable benchmarks.

This dilemma doesn't stop our industry from trying, though. There are many different ratios that can be created to compare security spend across multiple variables. For example:

- Percentage of IT budget allocated to security spend
- Cost of security per employee
- Security spending per (some dollar increment) of revenue
- Security full-time equivalencies (FTEs) as a percentage of total IT FTEs
- And many more…

Engaging in these metrics will indeed produce data points that can be compared to ratios from other organizations of similar size and industry. But consider the financial assumptions behind the data and one will recognize that there may be contributors to the benchmark data which diminish their effectiveness. For example, the percentage of IT budget dedicated to security spend assumes many factors. Because it is a point in time ratio, only measuring the current percentage at the time of the conversion, the numbers could be skewed as a result of security spend variability. If the ratio is taken in November after a February breach of the same year, the budget may reflect a large percentage of the IT budget that is allocated to security. This is normal after a large breach when new controls may be procured and implemented. However, in the previous year, the ratio may have been quite lower and as a result, this point in time ratio can be misleading. Using this example, the one-time ratio doesn't show a true trend in the security finances, only a reactive measurement, especially if future years show a decline in security funding.

Regarding the same ratio, it assumes that the IT budget is of adequate appropriateness. With so many IT departments reducing their budgets, it dilutes the security spend ratio with the assumption that with fewer IT costs, the necessity of security spend follows the same reductive path. Moreover, if the IT budget doesn't represent all the technology spend for a corporation, perhaps as a result of a de-centralized IT model with separate digital teams, eCommerce groups, etc., the ratio doesn't consider the security services provided to those separate technology teams (and security almost always provides services to the entire corporation, not just what is represented in IT).

Even with the challenges of utilizing ratios to understand security budget adequateness, they can still prove useful. Evaluating multiple ratios and doing so over time, looking for trends, can be effective in providing some actionable information. It isn't a perfect system that when data is put in, clear and final answers on how much to spend on security are provided. Deciding on how much to spend is very much like other business decisions, all with many variables to consider.

When a leadership team and board of directors are contemplating whether or not to buy a company, there isn't a system where information is entered and the decision to purchase or not purchase is spit out in seconds. Like security, many variables determine the likelihood of success that can influence the decision to invest or not. When acquiring a company, attributes such as valuation, customer base, company maturity, geographic considerations, the value it adds to the acquiring company, financial position, and the willingness to spend capital for the acquisition, etc., are just a few considerations. Even when the numbers reflect a potential positive outcome, there is still risk involved in making the decision.

Similarly, there are several variables that contribute to the choosing and purchasing of stock. Things like the individual's investment strategy, size of the company, product mix, pipeline, strategic outlook, and many others, all contribute to the decision-making process. In today's market, there is more data available to investors than ever before, with technologies that make trading accessible to so many. But in the end, these decisions may often rely on hunches that do not preclude risk. Even after exhaustive research on companies, a decision to invest in a specific stock doesn't guarantee substantial gains, if fact, one could realize large losses.

As with these examples, and many more, the decision to fund security can be fed with comparative data, yet there is still an element of risk involved in the investment decision. Better said, more security spend does not eliminate risk in the environment. As a matter of fact, even with substantial increases in your company's security budget, the company may still fall victim to a security breach (be it from an external source or through an insider attack) after those investments were made.

Budgeting security is not a "one and done" initiative; as mentioned previously, security cannot be looked upon like a project that has a completion. As threats evolve, security programs must evolve along with them to ensure the program retains its effectiveness. Other external factors could surface that require a re-alignment of security, such as emerging regulatory requirements or a breach of a large business partner.

Internal decisions could influence the current security posture, as well. There may be large shifts in the business strategy for the corporation, perhaps a decision to leverage more external partners in a large division of the company rather than investing in building the capability in-house, or maybe a substantial shift in the company's digital capabilities to create more omnichannel opportunities for customers. Each large shift requires a re-examination of the security capabilities to allow for the enablement of these transformative initiatives. And the earlier, the better.

Whatever the trigger of change, consistent and effective evaluation of the budgetary impacts for the security program will help to reduce the negative effects to the business. The CISO is a great resource to help navigate the business through such changes and explain the risk implications for following a particular strategic path. Asking questions of the CISO regarding how financial proposals for the security program are determined will provide you with needed information so that you may advise leadership appropriately.

BUILDING FINANCIAL PROPOSALS

Each budget proposal from the CISO most likely will include a justification for the required capability, costs, benchmarks, and perhaps some options. Often such proposals are followed by leadership requests seeking a return on investment (ROI) or defined value of the purchase from the CISO, however cyber security value is difficult to measure. While not impossible, there are methodologies available for the CISO to convert the purchase price of a security control into potential ROI calculations. Important to remember is that unlike traditional ROI, security ROI doesn't speak much to the financial return a company will enjoy but rather the likelihood of risk that it addresses or the expected security improvement it provides.

Potential attributes of a security ROI calculation could include avoidance costs:

- Revenue lost due to the incident
- Data loss costs, specifically trade secrets and regulatory data
- Losses related to brand reputation

The time that a CISO has with you can often be limited, so it is imperative that actionable information is shared and discussed within this allotted time. The aforementioned calculations provide data points that, on the surface, may provide a glimpse into specific financial impacts for a company, but all calculations rely on data points (and more importantly, the assumptions behind the data) to feed them. Because the director/CISO time together is so brief, I have found that describing these assumptions and all the underpinnings of the calculations takes time away from the core topics that aid the director in advising the company on cyber security matters. And in the end, the measurements don't visualize the realities of specific impacts to your company. The devil is in the details, and understanding them, particularly when making financial decisions on security resources, is critical.

Browse the Internet and you will find many different reports that relate to cyber security topics, most of which are extremely valuable in providing an industry view. Several cyber security vendors produce annual (sometimes more frequently) reports that outline threats and other areas they are seeing in the industry. Important to remember with these reports, as valuable as they are, is that they may leverage data from just the author's customer base (in other words, just a portion of the overall pool of available companies). There are think tanks and consultancies that deliver reports based on research, usually in the form of surveys and interviews, to provide industry numbers on a variety of cyber topics including security financials, i.e., the average cost of a breach, industries most financially impacted by a breach, etc. Diving into the research methodologies of the survey, one may find that a particular finding was based on surveying one thousand people in one specific geographical region (as an example). Understanding the particulars of the data and resulting findings is crucial in comparing the relevancy of them to your organization. Knowing the details of the survey, such as the number of respondents, title of the responding participants, do they have significant expertise in the area being surveyed, and other data points, can help translate the findings into which are valuable to leverage for decisions, as opposed to those findings that merely can be used as a conversation starter on the topic.

Additionally, many findings are averages for the participants of the study, leading to potential variability in the cost of a breach data point which can be dependent upon the size of the breach. Parameters may be set by the organization performing the study which explains such variability, which helps make the data clearer. The reports provide general guard rails for estimations based on the contributing data from the participating organizations being interviewed. Much like the published miles per gallon fuel consumption for your vehicle, your mileage (or cyber security measurements) may vary.

Security executives often leverage ratios that seek to quantify risks which are more specific to their company. Calculations such as annualized loss expectancy, probability of a security event, and a host of other, similar measurements often find their way into board presentations. With a desire to show clear, quantitative analysis of risk and how it applies to the company's security posture, the intent is worthy but only if all the underlying details behind the data are understood and considered when reviewing the ratios. As mentioned, the time for a CISO to brief a committee or board is limited and spending that time to debate the differences in predictability versus probability and other data inputs behind the figures may detract from the key issues. If used in combination with other justification factors, these computations may provide an additional, valuable data point, but on their own, I argue that funding or communicating a security program based solely on this type of analysis is not optimally effective.

Computations that seek to understand the impact on brand reputation are foggy as well. Few will argue (including me) that brands possess incredible value, some going back hundreds of years. There are many different types of valuations that help to measure brand value, with arguments on both sides related to the subjectivity of the analysis. My concerns for brand value relate to the ability in placing a specific dollar figure to the brand impact for a specific company who experiences a specific cyber security event.

Whatever methodology a company may use to determine brand value, pinpointing the impact of a breach on that value may be problematic. If brand valuation is dependent on the financial performance of the company, revenue generation, and competitive advantage to name a few, which of these metrics highlight the influence of a security event? Even in the face of the compelling timing associated with a breach, a downturn in revenue could also be attributed to many factors outside of a breach, perhaps a pricing increase, new offerings by a competitor, or a host of other variables. Attributing any financial impact to brand value solely on a cyber event may not be an accurate measurement. Simply put, and using the common Latin logical fallacy, *post hoc ergo propter hoc* ("after this, therefore because of this"), there could be more behind the numbers than just the data breach.

It is quite easy to conclude that breaches may cause significant financial distress for companies; I am a CISO, I would never suggest otherwise. However, there is a difference in stating that a breach impacts a company's brand value, versus attributing a specific cost to (or percentage of) the value of the brand, as a result of the attack. These are two very different things; one is a logical argument, and the other is a proposed measurement that may not be accurate for a particular company. It is important to reinforce that I am speaking to brand value in this section and not impacts to top-line revenue, market valuation, and bottom-line efficiencies – those figures are often quantifiable.

It may be true that a breach could involve diminishing consumer trust in a brand and as a result may have a negative influence on the brand image. With such deterioration of these brand attributes, it stands to reason that the value of the brand could be adversely affected. However, I suggest that designating a specific dollar amount to the brand value as a result of the breach is fundamentally flawed and may present a doomsday scenario without accurate (or actionable) data. All breaches are not equal, nor is each response to a breach. Each company has different nuances in the incident response process, and these can impact customer trust. If a company responds quickly, effectively, and are honest in communications around what took place, that is viewed much differently than a company that delays the response or worse, hides the facts surrounding the breach from its customers. Regulations on reporting help to keep all companies transparent to some degree, but I argue that how a company responds impacts consumer trust. And companies have varying effectiveness levels to responding to an incident. If these thoughts are true, it would suggest that attaching an average industry dollar amount around impact to brand value for *all* companies in the aggregate after a breach is flawed.

It is both wise and recommended that the CISO speaks to directors and leaders about the negative impacts to brand value that a breach can surface, however attempting to attach a dollar figure to that loss from an external, industry value will only drive more questions around the accuracy of the figure rather than actionable discussions regarding the core issue of protecting the brand.

My comments in this chapter may lead you to believe that industry reporting on security financials and other metrics are not helpful; this is not my intent. There is great value in these reports if used for what they are, broad ranges of data that provide a general baseline for the industry. Particularly useful is when they are used informationally in identifying trends year over year, such as general industry increases in the costs associated with recovering from a breach for example. Where I believe they are not as effective is when they are used as a primary data point that can be applied to each and every company.

There are other meaningful data that a CISO can present in building budgetary plans for funding a security strategy for their company. Data and measurements that are unique to the corporation are of the most value and these should be the calculations that the CISO leverages. As an analogous example, when reading the label on a bottle of medication, all the possible side effects associated with that medicine are listed in detail. It is important for all patients (the industry) to understand the potential side effects, but they are not an accurate measurement of what each patient will actually endure themselves. It may also be an important data point to understand what side effects family members (similar company size and revenue) had when taking the same medication. But the most valuable information is to understand what side effects the patient (the company) actually has when taking the medicine.

An excellent start for CISOs in this process is detailing the critical business processes that generate significant value for the company, and then outline the systems that support those processes. Armed with this information, several variants of measurement can be applied. The specific financial impact to the company by hour, day, week, etc., if one of these systems suffer a breach or outage, could be one such measurement. The CISO could report on the number of critical vulnerabilities within that system and if they are actively being exploited by adversaries in real-world situations (the active exploitation portion is a good example of when the industry reports mentioned above can provide real value). If the critical system provides manufacturing capabilities and suffers a breach, as we have seen in a few companies in recent years, an understanding of lost productivity by hourly or daily units could also be explored and reported. Inventory levels could be an effective measurement as well. If a company has a surplus of inventory and can measure how many days they can replenish customers after a breach, compared to a company with low inventory levels due to just in time manufacturing, this could provide valuable insight for the board. An example of supply chain impacts and subsequent shortages that comes to my mind is during the height of the recent pandemic, how many of us entered a grocery store and went straight to the isle with toilet tissue and hand sanitizer?

If a goal for the strategic plan includes increased labor costs specific to monitoring the corporate environment for incidents and threats, a combination of external and internal data can help justify the need for this enhanced business resiliency. Presenting industry findings by organizations who specialize in threat intelligence and study the capabilities of formalized adversary groups helps to show data on average times associated with adversaries breaking into networks. Using this time-based data on adversary capabilities, the CISO then measures their own current detection capabilities (how long it takes the team to detect and remediate an incident) and then overlays that capability against the industry benchmarks. For example, an industry report may highlight that it takes a particular type of adversary a certain number of minutes to enter a network and begin lateral movement. The CISO then displays the organization's current capabilities to detect and remediate threats. Using these metrics often can help to identify gaps and explain how the increased labor requests (or outsourcing) could aid in closing those gaps, enabling the security team to help get business processes back up and running in the event of a security incident. Of course, other metrics can be used to show the financial comparisons to building an internal monitoring capability versus outsourcing to a trusted partner.

Ensuring that all stakeholders are aligned on the financial strategy for security prevents future misunderstandings that could delay program progress. Leaders and directors should ask detailed questions of their CISO regarding each justification data point. In some cases, measurements may be used that seem to highlight good business sense, but when diving into the details, the intent of the data may be misconstrued – particularly in the area of cost savings. An example of this misconstrued intent is when a requestor wishes to buy a technology and mentions one of the positive outcomes for the purchase is labor cost savings. They may say that the addition of the technology, while an increase to the budget, will provide cost savings in labor, the equivalent of two FTEs annually for example, due to the automation that the technology provides.

This justification may make good business sense for the company and leadership approves the request, the technology is procured, and installed. Then the business leaders return to rightly question: when can we enjoy those cost savings by removing the funds for those two FTEs from the security budget, and either (a) recognize the savings, or (b) re-allocate the savings to another business initiative? The requestor frantically explains that the intent was not to reduce the labor budget for the team by two FTEs; it was to simply state that it would save labor costs so that two team members can divert their efforts to more critical job functions. This isn't a cost savings; it is actually adding cost (with some potentially new service capabilities for the diverted efforts). If the intent was to indeed reduce the labor budget by two, then the justification is accurate. It seems straightforward; however, I wouldn't have included this example if I've not seen this type of inaccurate cost saving justification used by others on several occasions. Aligning on the intent of each justification helps to avoid future confusion.

A combination of external and internal data points, with a bias for internally relevant information, is the optimal method for a CISO to build financial proposals. Too heavy of a reliance on external data takes away from company-specific information and may provide inaccurate numbers. Leaning too heavily on internal data may lead to creating a program in a vacuum that isn't industry relevant. The goal is for the measurements to support decision-making, without significant time in debating or questioning the appropriateness of the data.

Clarifying the types of investments, be it capital expenditures or operating expense, for each of the security budget line items is an important aspect of the CISO's financial strategic plan and should be included in the discussion with leadership. There may be benefits for each of the options and is largely dependent on the company's financial strategy, preferences, and regulations related to capitalization versus operating expense. As a result, ensuring the CISO's plan is closely aligned with these corporate goals and preferences are important and should be explored in the strategy discussion.

TIMING OF INVESTMENTS

Funding every needed security investment all at once may not be possible (or desired) for many corporations. Balancing many factors such as available resources for executing projects, large gaps in specific areas of the company's security posture, or perhaps the financial position to fund security projects ensures a solid plan in which to build the security program. To achieve this balance, the CISO may start with the most critical needs first, then work through other initiatives later in the strategic plan. By leveraging the completed assessment, prioritization can be communicated using a simple visual to represent the order of project needs (see Figure 8.1).

The prioritization of security initiatives most likely will remain somewhat consistent in the short- and mid-term plan, but directors and leaders should be aware of potential adjustments when the plan is being executed. Because both threats and business evolve so rapidly, flexibility in the plan is essential. When advancements in detection or vulnerability management are approved for the security organization, for example, the next logical after-effect is the organization beginning to detect more opportunities to enhance the security posture of the company. This shift may be a result of not having

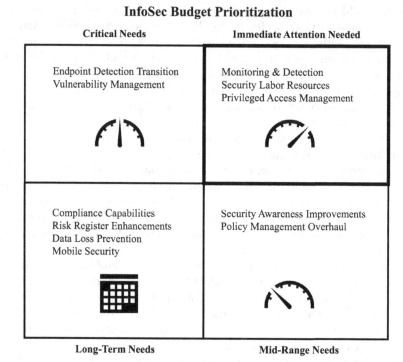

Figure 8.1 InfoSec budget prioritization.

the enhanced detection capabilities in the past but with increased visibility now. Subsequently, there is the possibility that a cyber security initiative is added to the list that was not present previously in the initial plan.

Information security finances play an important role in building the security program for the company. Too much funding may lead to cost inefficiencies and too little may open up the company to risk that could otherwise be reduced. Leveraging a combination of internally heavy data, complimented with external industry insights, helps to navigate the difficult tasks of finding a proper balance while ensuring other corporate initiatives continue to progress.

Chapter 9

The role of security vendors and consultants

Depending on the analysis you may read from a variety of sources, the number of current cyber security companies can range anywhere between approximately 3000 and 50,000. For our purposes here, let's just agree that the number of companies providing some variation of cyber security products and/or services is massive. To be sure, it is a hot market with new start-ups springing up every year. As a CISO, I average roughly sixteen unsolicited vendor emails on my work account each day; four connection requests on social media daily from cyber security company's sales representatives; eight phone calls from salespersons on my personal phone each day; and four daily phone calls on my work phone line. Each one with a request to tell me more about how their technology can strengthen my company's security posture. It is truly an active market and there is simply not enough time for a CISO to answer each request.

To help address this time constraint, I categorize security companies into three segments: vendors, partners, and extensions of my team. Vendors are those that I do not currently do business with, but I keep an eye on their emerging capabilities. Partners are those firms I leverage to some degree in my security program. Lastly, those companies that provide critical support to my security organization and work hard at nurturing the working relationships are ones that I consider to be extensions of my team.

Companies rely on cyber security providers to assist them in combating threats, and the technologies they provide are an integral part to an information security program. Selecting those technologies, as well as their providers, can be a daunting task if there isn't a structured process in place for determining selection. Prior to any discussions with vendors, the CISO should already understand their needs for a particular security technology and a basic understanding of the attributes desired, so that focused vendor discussions can take place. For example, when walking into a car dealership, customers don't say, "Show me everything; I want to see it all – electric vehicles, trucks, compact cars, vans, sports cars, sedans, and SUV's". No, instead the consumer already has an idea of one or two types

DOI: 10.1201/9781003477341-11

of vehicles they want to explore, maybe the color they desire and a general understanding of a price range they can expect to pay for the vehicle. With a similar understanding of needed security attributes, the CISO can be better positioned to choose the right technology and vendor.

UNDERSTANDING DESIRED ATTRIBUTES

There are specific attributes to every security technology purchase. Attributes such as product performance, service after the sale support, interoperability with other technologies, price, and a host of others, each of which have varying levels of importance for the purchaser (the more a product matches the needed attributes, the better). No one attribute should be weighted so heavily that it ignores many of the other desired features. For example, a very low-cost solution may be an incredibly attractive attribute on its own, but it loses that appeal if the product isn't of the appropriate quality and lacks many other attributes required to effectively address specific threats. The cost may be good, but the value is not.

An effective way to understand which technology and vendor to leverage is through effective planning. One recommendation is for the CISO to assemble the appropriate stakeholders to discuss the approved strategic initiative and identify the specific needs for the technology that addresses the strategic initiative. Bringing together all affected parties, in small groups or as one large team, ensures that everyone can raise important characteristics that contribute to an effective technology selection. Most of the time, these stakeholders will include non-security team members.

Documentation is key to ensure that attributes are clearly defined. As an example, if a CISO is looking to add a security awareness platform, some potential areas for the team to explore are partially outlined in Figure 9.1.

Once the criteria have been established by the collective stakeholders, a popular additional step is to rank the different attributes within each of the categories of *critical needs, should have,* and *nice to have.* A simple system can be effective to label which attributes are the most important within each category.

The CISO can then research the different capabilities of vendors in the desired technology space. Research firms, consultancies, online forums, and industry peers are very good sources for discovering which products and vendors lead in that technology vertical. However, this information serves merely as a data point because each technology deployment and experience are unique to each company.

Armed with this information, the CISO and team are only now ready to begin talking with targeted vendors. Each discussion is usually comprised of an account representative and technical sales support person from the vendor, who both dive into the capabilities of the product, provide

Vendor Attribute Priorities

Needed Attribute	Explanation	Critical Need (CN) Should Have (SH) Nice to Have (NTH)
Interoperability: Employee Training Tracking	Can leverage existing systems to attribute specific employees, region, organization, and job role, to the specific training.	CN
Interoperability: Email	Functions appropriately with current email security platform.	CN
Dynamic Testing: Campaign Delivery	Provides the ability to send internal phishing campaigns to employees.	CN
Dynamic Testing: Customized Campaign	Ability to customize phishing campaigns.	CN
Dynamic Testing: Language Support	Phishing campaigns can be translated to multiple languages inside the platform.	SH
Dynamic Testing: Reporting	Robust reporting capabilities on user phishing performance by region, business unit, and system type.	CN
Cost	Competitive price for platform, initial and recurring, and support options.	SH
Enhanced Functionality: Removeable Media Awareness	USB thumb drives to place in corporate locations to test users on using unknown devices.	NTH

Figure 9.1 Vendor attribute priorities.

demonstrations, and answer questions. During these discussions, each team member can fill out an internal form developed to note how they believe the product matches the prioritized list of needs. Again, documentation in this stage helps to clarify product selection and what follows (leveraging the same security awareness example from above) is one option for tracking information from the vendor meetings. The needed attributes are listed in the first column, with the other columns devoted to each vendor. Outputs from the individual vendor meetings are scored, perhaps 1–5, with 1 being the highest score available and 5 meaning a low correlation to the needed attribute. If the vendor does not possess a particular defined attribute, these may be referenced with the label zero (see Figure 9.2).

The internal team meets again to discuss the results, compare scores, and highlights key take-aways from each vendor meeting. Completing all this preliminary work can be a significant task, but the value in doing so helps to reduce future problems that may arise. I've included the details of this structure within these pages so that you may understand a potential process for product selection, and then can ask the CISO about the methodology they used in purchasing security products and services. Ensuring that thoughtful analysis was performed by the CISO will give you confidence that product choices were not merely based on cost, personal bias, or other unstructured elements.

Vendor Scoring Sheet

Needed Attribute	Vendor #1 Name	Vendor #2 Name	Vendor #3 Name
Interoperability: Employee Training Tracking	1	2	1
Interoperability: Email	2	0	1
Dynamic Testing: Campaign Delivery	1	4	2
Dynamic Testing: Customized Campaign	3	5	1
Dynamic Testing: Language Support	3	0	2
Dynamic Testing: Reporting	1	2	1
Cost	2	1	3
Enhanced Functionality: Removeable Media Awareness	3	4	3

Figure 9.2 Vendor scoring.

OUTSOURCING SECURITY

With increasing regulations, breaches, and the emergence of cyber security as a critical enabler of corporate business, in contrast with the available resources within the security industry, attracting and hiring experienced security talent has been challenging for some time. To address this, many security vendors have implemented services that provide full labor support (as a service) for their specific security platforms to alleviate the burden of clients hiring an FTE to perform this task. At first glance, this may appear to be an appealing alternative to solve a real labor constraint. Directors should dive more deeply into the decision to take advantage of these services, as well as the justification process for making the decision in these cases. It may be the case that a security platform vendor offers a support service for $200,000 U.S. annually (as an example) for supporting *only* their technology offering. If the estimate is an accurate representation of the costs associated with the service, it may not make good financial sense for a company. The price of that limited service could potentially fund two entry-level internal FTEs (fully burdened) for the security program who could support the particular platform, as well as supporting other cyber security initiatives. If a security organization leverages more than one of these vendor service offerings, the collective value could diminish even more.

Other vendors may provide dedicated resources to a client in the area of (again, as an example) threat intelligence. This resource would be committed to the client and provide very specialized services in garnering threat intelligence and reporting on them for the company. Since attracting and hiring a Threat Intelligence Specialist can be very difficult, and expensive, this type of service may make good fiscal sense for the company.

Lastly, companies have built Managed Security Services Provider (MSSP) services. The vendor provides services to monitor and respond to cyber threats on behalf of the client, leveraging an operational model with security operation centers that may be sprinkled across the globe to provide 24x7x365 services. In the past decade, these providers have added more specialized services to their suite of capabilities such as forensics and incident response to round out their catalog.

So how can you ensure that the CISO is choosing the right services to outsource, and which are appropriate to build in-house? It should come as no surprise when the answer is "it depends on the company", as that is the common theme throughout this book. However, there are some tips and things to look for when making the outsourcing decision.

The first is the need for expediency. To build capabilities in cyber security takes time to post jobs, attract talent, interview, make final candidate selections, background checks, and onboarding the new person. Leveraging outsourced services can help by standing up services quickly, especially when it comes to incident response (more on this topic later). If significant time constraints are present, it may make sense to outsource a specific capability, even if it is to only supplement the time it takes to build the capability internally.

Next, it is important to consider the level of specialization needed to perform a specific task. Mentioned earlier were services such as threat intelligence and forensics, to name just two. For small- to medium-sized corporations, it may not make sense to build out such capabilities using internal resources and incur those costs when the company can leverage established, on-demand services provided by leading experts in the field.

Evaluating the tasks being done by your in-house team to understand the engagement desires of the internal staff is also a very important consideration. Security experts with five or more years of experience may not feel fully engaged or may feel they are not participating in work they consider to be of high value, if they are merely monitoring network traffic looking for threats. They entered the field to perform engaging, highly technical work – tasks that provide them with challenge and self-fulfillment. In the absence of this type of work, the company may incur higher turnover of cyber security personnel who move on to other opportunities that provide more engaging work.

One of the largest factors to consider in outsourcing is cost, or better stated, the value of the investment in outsourced services. Building an internal capability to provide 24x7x365 monitoring services can be quite a large investment for a company. There are direct costs associated with the labor required to provide such continuous monitoring for the company. Whether the staff is assembled in one location or spread across points all over the globe with the appropriate shift hand-offs, labor costs associated with building this important capability should be analyzed extensively. An internal capability will include the monitoring employees, shift supervisors, managers, and potentially a site director to run the program. Plans should be made to ensure there is an adequate number of staff to account for vacations, time-off, and time zone differences – if operating in multiple regions. CISOs should be cognizant of any gaps in coverage when switching monitoring services from site to site. Due to transferring the detection duties between global locations, there may be cases when a slight time frame exists where monitoring may not occur; potentially weekends and holidays, even if only for an hour. And in reviewing industry trends of when adversaries seek to attack, one will find it is often on weekends and holidays. Confirming the headcount that is appropriate to eliminate any gaps of coverage is vital, and management may find the results to be potentially expensive.

Aside from the direct labor costs, there may be other expenses that surface to support such an internal model. For example, if the monitoring team(s) will be in a corporate office(s), there are required expenses to ensure the appropriate facility services are available, such as heating/cooling, security guards, and cafeteria/food services (when many offices may reduce these services outside of normal business hours).

As an alternative to in-house development of detection services, several vendors have implemented an MSSP capability to provide monitoring (and other) services to clients which offer 24x7x365 coverage at a rate that can be much less than a company building its own ability. By leveraging economies of scale, the MSSP can monitor corporate networks and alert their clients to potential threats at a much lower cost. This relieves the client from incurring the expense of standing up an internal program while providing continuous monitoring around the clock. With the benefits of an outsourced monitoring contract comes a few watch items that should be considered when deciding to move such an important aspect of your information security program to a third party.

First, not all MSSPs are considered equal. There are medium- and large-sized security corporations that specialize in cyber security and whose capabilities are best of breed. At the same time, there are very small vendors who offer similar services but without the focused competencies in cyber security. In the past decade, the industry has seen emerging offerings from small- and medium-sized consultancies who are very good in some domains but may lack the expertise in detecting threats. Using the same criteria previously mentioned for determining the most important needs in an outsourced relationship, companies should evaluate the breadth and, importantly, the depth of the services provided by each of the vendor candidates.

No matter which MSSP is chosen, it is important to remember that the vendor is providing baseline services to multiple clients. It is unlikely that a third party will have the same intimate knowledge of your corporate network, the company's business processes and strategies, or who are all the key stakeholders across IT and the business. Even with an outsourced model, the CISO still needs to build a capable, internal team of security professionals to investigate alerts, translate them into realistic threats to your organization, and remediate them. Much like a cloud outsourcing model, security cannot be fully proxied to a third party with the expectation that a full-service security program will follow. A strong relationship between the service provider and the client is vital. Ensuring that service levels are agreed upon, open communication between the two entities is well established, and actionable metrics/alerts are provided to the client helps in this assurance. This relationship, unlike many others, is truly an extension of the internal team.

MSSPs are a considerable target for adversaries with the hope that in breaching the provider's infrastructure, the threat actor may be able to traverse to client networks. Significant resources from Nation-state adversaries are focused on these suppliers with this goal in mind and while cyber security focused MSSPs deploy significant controls to protect their offering, the increased targeting is a consideration to be weighed in deciding on which partner a company should engage to perform their monitoring services.

Cyber security vendors have expanded their portfolio of services that extend well beyond detection. As mentioned earlier, there may be cases in which highly experienced outsourced partners can be a good alternative to building these non-monitoring, highly technical services within your company. But as with most things, an argument can be made where building internal capabilities may make good financial sense, particularly for large corporations. As I write this, I have seen hourly rates for vendors providing deep security analysis services ranging from $300 to $600 (U.S. dollars). If a large enterprise has a high demand for these niche services on an ongoing basis, the CISO could rightly argue that they are able to do it at an internal rate of $70–$150 per hour, fully burdened, along with some technology additions, and potentially some specialized training for the security staff. Speaking of the security employees, this deep and challenging work is what they want to do – it is why they entered the field.

CISOs require assistance in carrying out their duties, and security vendors are an important part of building a holistic security program. At the same time, the security product/service industry has saturated executives with marketing, making it difficult to decipher which partner/tools to select to enrich our internal security postures and at a value-added cost. With solid preparation, research, and documentation, the CISO can maneuver through this uncertainty and increase their chances of finding the right solution at the right price, and with a partner who can be considered an extension of the internal security team.

Chapter 10

Security service management

It may be quite easy to conjure up an image of a corporate cyber security team and the way they carry out their important duties each day. If the stereotypical image comes to mind, no doubt they are assembled somewhere (either virtually or in an office) secretly performing "behind the curtain" functions that few outside of the team are aware of. While this is an exaggerated view (many security teams have evolved from this typecast), delivering cyber security services is indeed a novel concept that isn't easily understood. Promoting the team as an enabler of the business and showcasing the services that are provided to the enterprise are great ways to shine light on this functional area that historically may have operated in the dark. We'll discuss this more in the chapter on security awareness. For our purposes in this chapter, we'll review the importance of service delivery for an information security organization and what it means for those outside the cyber team.

Directors should seek out details in the security strategy that highlight the operating capabilities for the cyber security organization. A good way to demonstrate these capabilities is through a strong security service management program created by the CISO and their team. The program highlights its activities and explains the delivery and ongoing operations for each of its capabilities. In doing so, employees outside of the security organization can better understand how the security organization supports them. What follows are some general tips and guidelines that have proven successful for me across different companies. Remember that this is general information to enable the director to ask questions of the plan for his or her company and should not be seen as a complete service management program with all the elements that a professional in the service management field could provide. We'll leave that to those experts. What follows is more than enough though to show the importance of a basic service management program for cyber security and its benefits.

Leveraging the organizational structure of the security organization, each service tower consists of several buckets of service areas. For example, if one of

DOI: 10.1201/9781003477341-12

Security Service Towers

Security Operations		Governance, Risk, & Compliance		Identity Access Mgmt	
Vulnerability Management	Endpoint Security	Policy Management	Security Awareness	Multi-Factor Authentication	Privileged Access
Server/System Security	Monitoring & Detection	Compliance	Risk Management	Federation & Single Sign-On	Identity Access Lifecycle
Cloud Security	Application Security			ERP Security	Architecture Services
OT/IoT Security	Threat Intelligence			Data Loss Prevention	IAM Governance

Figure 10.1 Security service towers.

the teams is security operations, potential buckets could include vulnerability management, endpoint security, monitoring/detection, server/system security, cloud security, application security, OT/IoT security, threat intelligence, and penetration testing, to name a few possible examples. Another team may be focused on governance, risk, and compliance (GRC) and its buckets may include security awareness, risk management, policy management, metrics, third-party risk, and possibly compliance. How many service towers exist is dependent on the company, but the above areas serve as a good sample for our purposes here. When assembled, the service towers may look as in Figure 10.1.

Each block within each service tower represents a bucket of services, with each block containing five to ten discrete services related to the service area. For example, under GRC there is a block called "security awareness", and within that block contains individual services such as role-based training, annual security compliance training, security awareness articles, internal phishing campaigns, reporting, as well as other potential services. It is important to capture as many of the services the team provides and after identifying all the services within all the buckets across the different security towers, an information security service catalog begins to emerge.

The next step is to create a work breakdown structure (WBS) that breaks down the enormous work areas performed by the cyber security team into manageable increments. A standard numbering system is sufficient to group smaller services with the larger service buckets within the security service tower. For example:

1.0 GRC Services
    1.1 Security Awareness
        1.1.1   Role-Based Training
        1.1.2   Annual Security Compliance Training
        1.1.3   Security Awareness Articles
        1.1.4   Internal Phishing Campaigns

With the foundations in place, the service catalog is ready to be built out through the creation of service descriptions for *each* discrete service. Although they could vary depending on need, potential elements of the service descriptions could include the following.

SERVICE NAME

As it suggests, this is the name of the service. Because the service catalog is geared for non-security personnel, industry or very technical terms should be avoided. For example, a service name should not be Static Application Security Testing. Instead, leveraging a simple descriptor such as Software Security Testing may be easier for readers to understand. Within the service description, any differentiation between the specific types of software testing can be explained.

SHORT DESCRIPTION

This is a quick reference for the user to understand a summary of the service. Containing a few sentences, the short description provides an executive overview of the service being documented.

LONG DESCRIPTION

Expanding on the short description, this section highlights more specifics related to the service, what is included, and a brief highlight of the steps involved in providing the service. Keeping with the security awareness example, and specifically role-based training, some of the steps could include the identification of training participants by role, curriculum development, creation of presentation materials, resource allocation steps (booking rooms or video conferencing), delivery of the training curriculum, reporting on who attended the training, and so on. The long service description provides all the details of what is included in the service so that delivery outcomes are clearly understood by all stakeholders.

SERVICE LEVEL OBJECTIVE (SLO)

All relative timelines and expected quality of service results are included in this section. It highlights the components of what the final delivery product/service/report will include, timelines associated with the service, and appropriate measurements related to examining the effectiveness of the service. For some security organizations, particularly those that are in the building stage and not as mature as they would like to be, there may be a hesitance to commit to specific service levels knowing that they cannot meet them with current resources. I understand this reluctance, but by providing SLOs that outline where the security organization wants to be in a particular service area, measurements can be gathered to assist in resource planning. Rather than approaching senior leadership with labor addition requests that are justified by "we have a lot of work in this area and are falling behind" – a more effective method exists. By drawing a line in the sand with target SLOs, the CISO can show the average number of hours it takes to provide the service effectively, the current state of SLO performance, the gap between the two, and the labor resources needed to close the gap. This data-driven analysis can be achieved through the SLO component of the service catalog and provides excellent justification for resources.

HOW TO ORDER THE SERVICE

An important part of any service catalog is how a user orders the services from the information security team for the particular statement of work. Ordering the service may involve a ticketing system so that all services are tracked from order to completion or perhaps a request to a centralized corporate email box. Whatever method a company uses, the specifics for how to order the service are outlined in this section. On more than a few occasions, a cyber security service won't involve the customer ordering the service, instead it is just something that is pushed out by the security team, i.e., network monitoring. This doesn't negate the need for a service description and details such as these should be included in this section of the service catalog.

COST OF THE SERVICE

Not all companies allocate security costs by services provided. Some may do a general security allocation based on the number of employees or by email accounts, and others may do no allocation at all. Even without a cost allocation model, capturing the internal costs associated with providing the service can be beneficial in future demand management forecasting. This section of the service description highlights the labor costs for the time anticipated in providing the service, plus any additional internal or external costs that may be incurred in its delivery.

It has been outlined previously that security services are more cost effective and with fewer project schedule delays when the information security team is brought into the initiative during its earliest stages. To help promote this, the service catalog highlights the varying levels of a service available to the requestor, possibly in the form of standard, gold, and platinum services. For example, if a requestor would like a vulnerability scan of a specific system tied to one of their critical processes, the standard service option may detail that the scan and subsequent reporting of results will take five business days. In some cases, the requestor may explain the service is just what they need, but they require it to be completed in three days. Security can still provide the service, but this gold level requires a 2x multiplier to the standard labor cost associated with the service. Perhaps the requestor would like the service, but time restrictions require the service to be completed in one business day. This platinum service includes a 3x multiplier to the standard labor cost due to the aggressive schedule. We see this type of service option when we order products online and are contemplating shipping options. There are standard shipping times, as well as a host of other options up to and including next day air, that deliver the product according to the consumer's need. However, the product ordered is still the same. Incorporating these levels in a company that allocates costs based on services helps to incentivize earlier engagement of security. For those companies that do not do such allocation, this level of detail is still a benefit for planning purposes related to demand management by looking at trending data of how services are typically ordered and on what timeline.

SERVICE OPTIONS

For an information security service, typically there are no alternative options available (or permitted) for the person requesting services. A requestor cannot leverage a third party of their choice to perform security offerings in a chartered information security program because the cyber security organization has been authorized by the executive leadership team as the sole provider of security services for the company. In a few cases, a particular business unit or functional area may require a third party to perform a penetration test to meet certain requirements, contractual or regulatory, as an example. In such cases, this section of the service catalog outlines that the information security organization serves as the sole facilitator of the external service, working with the external provider to generate the penetration test – usually a trusted partner that the security team uses frequently. The business unit should not engage security services on their own, without interaction with the core information security organization.

Even with security services that are mandated with no service options, the service catalog provides good transparency for company employees into the functions that the cyber security organization delivers. Additionally, it is a great data point for CISOs in their demand management planning.

DEPENDENT SERVICES

The ability to provide a service in most disciplines requires assistance from others and depends on other service providers. Information security is no different and this section of the service description outlines those dependent services. For example, a service offered by security may be to perform an online forensic capture of a particular computer – which requires Internet connectivity, and Internet connectivity isn't something that information security provides as a service – they rely on the IT network team to provide that capability. In the case of a company leveraging an MSSP, the security team relies on that partner to provide baseline services. When building SLOs for the internal service it is important that the internal team understands the SLOs from those dependent services and takes those into consideration in the SLO performance of their own service.

Once all the service descriptions have been completed for the cyber security organization, the final step is to publish the service catalog. An important consideration in doing so is to ensure that the catalog is accessible to the broader company and not isolated in the technology organization. Wider visibility provides all corners of the business with awareness to the important services that security provides to enable the business.

The value of creating and publishing a service management program for information security may not be immediately apparent, potentially looked upon as an administrative task that may not have relevancy to a company that doesn't engage in formalized service delivery. However, by establishing a security service management program, the CISO can obtain valuable information on the most (and least) used services in the organization, the performance of the team in delivering those services, and a glimpse into demand management that could potentially assist with future planning.

At the very least, such inquiries of the CISO about service delivery can produce insights for you on how the security program provides services for the company.

OPERATIONAL CADENCE AND THE RHYTHM OF SECURITY OPERATIONS

While the service catalog focuses on the consumers of security services, there is an additional need for an internal program designed for the cyber security team that documents the operational cadence of the cyber security program. This operating model helps to clarify roles and responsibilities, internal processes, and instructions on how the cyber security organization conducts its operations. Above all else, it retains the information in a centralized place so that the documentation is readily available to all members of the team, helping to reduce single points of failure. The operational model can include multiple types of sections derived from what is important for the CISO to capture. Some examples may include the following.

PEOPLE

Documenting the people aspects of the cyber security team adds value insofar as it explains each security employee's expertise in certain areas, role, responsibilities, perhaps core competencies in specific security technologies, training updates, and more. It may also include contact information, certifications, and information that makes it easier for other security employees to understand who they can reach out to with questions or assistance with various tasks and details about specific security technologies.

Equally important is to detail the experts outside of the information security organization, possibly from the IT team. Examples could include network administrators, email administrators, database experts, cloud infrastructure points of contact, and many more. To help thank the different non-security groups for providing their contact/expertise information, the CISO can give the other teams the established roster of the information security team that outlines expertise in the various security areas.

PROCESS

Whether it is how to respond to specific tasks or the proper method for configuring a system, documenting the security processes helps to maintain consistency in operations no matter who from the team is performing the process. Step-by-step instructions are documented for various situations, examples may include business email compromise, data theft, device misconfiguration, denial of service incident, lost or stolen device, privilege escalation, suspicious network activity, and a host of others.

The format is flexible, the documentation can take the form of a Wiki[1], or perhaps formal documentation in a data repository – all of which are secured with strong access controls, up to potentially leveraging multi-factor authentication.

TECHNOLOGY

With so many different types of security technologies in use at your company, it is imperative that information is retained for each one. Some data that may provide value in the operational model could include:

- General information on the technology
- Whitepapers, research, and industry reports from the vendor
- Contact information for the vendor, account rep, technical support, etc.
- Copies of the contract/renewal
- Implementation notes from the professional services team
- Configuration data

In doing so, the information is readily available to the entire team rather than residing on one person's computer.

DATABASE OF INFORMATION

A perennial activity for most cyber security teams is answering a questionnaire for any variety of purposes. It may be for compliance reasons, cyber insurance policies, or perhaps general questions about the infrastructure size/type for scoping exercises when exploring new technology purchases. Rather than treating each questionnaire individually by assembling a team to research the answers, I have found that a one-to-many approach is much more efficient. The questions and answers are entered into a database of responses, always available, and can be leveraged to answer multiple types of inquiries. If new questions are asked that do not have a response, they are added to the database. Following this methodology means that only at regular intervals, perhaps annually or after a large change in the corporate infrastructure, the responses are checked to ensure they remain accurate.

Value can also be found in storing reference architectures. These architectures provide a baseline approach to implementing a system and may include diagrams, process flowcharts, and other types of reference materials. Lastly, industry documentation such as common frameworks is a valuable addition to the operational model.

The formalization of service management and operational cadence lends themselves to effective, efficient, and repeatable processes for the cyber security organization. Each program takes significant time to build, but the results are worth the effort. Even without such programs, it is important for the director to inquire about the structure of security operations to ensure that these services are not performed on an ad hoc basis and instead, follow rigorous standardization.

Note

1   An online resource, publicly accessible or solely internal to an organization, that holds data, knowledge, and can be edited by multiple users.

Chapter 11

A vision for cyber security board governance

An argument can be made about the need for increased board-level cyber security involvement by merely arguing the benefits to the business. Implementing preventative controls, continuous monitoring, and the ability to respond to cyber events in a timely manner, all contribute to the effectiveness of a company's ability to manufacture products, ship them, deliver services, and transact with their customers.

Good cyber security makes good business sense.

Many corporations understand this and have implemented impressive cyber security programs without any direct regulations. Some have even created dedicated cyber security committees as part of their board structure. They have woven security into the rhythm of the business and look to cyber as an enabler of the business rather than a hindrance to it, or a necessary compliance requirement.

A portion of these companies have built these impressive security functions on their own accord. They see the cyber security program in a visionary way, understanding the value in creating a robust capability for their business. Other companies may have built a cyber security program in which few others can compare, investing millions in the security budget, but have done so only after a major breach – when the realization of not having such a program becomes relevant for them. For some other companies, imposed regulations to increase cyber capabilities serve as the only driver for improvement.

At the time of this writing, there are final rules by the U.S. Securities and Exchange Commission (U.S. SEC)[1] being implemented that seek to enhance and standardize disclosures regarding cyber security risk management, strategy, governance, and incident reporting by public companies. I believe there is an important distinction between the value of enhancing cyber security oversight by a company on its own accord and the value of implementing enhancements after being mandated to disclose its cyber security oversight. As mentioned, an effective cyber security program is good business and can be an enabler to it. I began writing this book a year

DOI: 10.1201/9781003477341-13

prior to the SEC initially proposing the draft rules with the notion that cyber security oversight needed to be enhanced. Today, not only does effective cyber security oversight make good business sense, the disclosure of certain elements of a company's cyber program now require it.

The rules require, among other things,

> current reporting about material cyber security incidents and periodic reporting to provide updates about previously reported cyber security incidents. The rules also require periodic reporting about a registrant's processes to identify and manage cyber security risks; the registrant's board of directors' oversight of cyber security risk; and management's role and expertise in assessing and managing cyber security risk.

One of the rules that did not make the final requirements was the proposed rule for "annual reporting or certain proxy disclosures about the board of directors' cyber security expertise, if any".[2]

The final rules require more disclosure around various aspects of a public company's cyber security program than ever previously required. Implicant then would be the notion that a company's leadership, including its board of directors, understands these various aspects of their cyber program enough to have the ability to disclose them. Rather than repeat each of the SEC rules in this book, perhaps our time would best be served by examining the potential impacts, as well as some commentary from my perspective that may provide value for you in your oversight duties?

As with any rule or regulation, time is needed to understand how they will affect real-world scenarios. Some may find initial ambiguity in terms such as "substantial likelihood" or "reasonable shareholder", to name just two, but perhaps with time and application of the rules to real events, more clarity of the definitions will emerge. While there are foundations in place to determine the materiality of corporate issues, I believe materiality too may require more discussion across boards and management teams as it relates to cyber incidents. The intent of the rules, however, is very clear, to enhance elements of cyber security reporting for a publicly traded company to better inform investors.

BOARD OVERSIGHT

In many companies, cyber security updates are already integrated into full board and/or committee meetings. For those organizations where they are not fully integrated, the final rules will require disclosure of the board's oversight of material risks from cyber security threats, and, if applicable, identify any board committee or subcommittee responsible for such oversight.

Even within those companies where a regular cadence of cyber security conversations is already established, the rules would require disclosure of the oversight, perhaps necessitating a need to enhance what is already being done.

Consider the proposed item 106(c)(2) that requires specific disclosure of how management reports to the board or a committee on material cyber security risk. In the final amendments, the SEC published its intent that the purpose of the rules, including at proposal, was to inform investors and not to influence whether and how companies manage their cyber security risk.[3] It is my belief, however, that the natural byproduct of such a disclosure is it will indeed indirectly entice boards to elevate the cyber discussion, lest they be seen as devoting just enough time on cyber security or perhaps not doing as much as peers (or competitors) in their industry. Peer review is a very strong motivator.

At one point in my career, I led the cyber security program for one of the several operating sectors of a large corporation. Each quarter, leadership would travel to the different sector sites for all day sessions that dove into the projects, financials, and performance of the sector's IT organization, which included cyber security. Metrics on a wide range of topics were shared and those measurements drove the conversations. A metric would be displayed on the conference room screen, perhaps the number of critical vulnerabilities for all sectors, and inevitably each sector representative would quickly scan the chart for their own sector. How many critical vulnerabilities did they have in their sector that quarter? How did their sector perform in patching those vulnerabilities? And of particular importance, how did their sector compare to all of their other peer sectors? The impact of sharing comparative information, as used in this example, I believe, is the same type of influence that we'll see to some degree when companies begin to disclose the general oversight of their company's cyber security program.

The final SEC rules, after consideration of the public comments, removed the proposition for disclosing a registrant board of directors' cyber security expertise. It was determined that cyber security processes are completed at the management level and that board members with broad-based skills in risk management and strategy can effectively oversee the cyber security program "without specific subject matter expertise, as they do with other sophisticated technical matters".[4]

While the proposed rule was dropped, I believe that our industry will ultimately see a similar requirement for disclosing board members with cyber security expertise at some point in the future. Even without a specific mandate, I believe more boards will have someone with cyber security expertise within its ranks. Whether it is externally or internally motivated, I predict this for a few reasons:

1. There is a distinction to be made with the term 'subject matter expertise'. While it is true that many directors may not have specific subject matter expertise in cyber security, an overall, general

understanding of the domain *is* required to perform oversight. As an analogy, a particular director on a board may not have deep, subject matter expertise in finance or served as a CFO for a corporation – instead, perhaps their expertise lies in manufacturing or supply chain operations. However, this particular director will indeed have a general understanding of the finance domain and can read/understand a balance sheet and all the associated financial measurements in order to contribute to the fiscal conversations and consultation to the management team. For those special oversight responsibilities that rely on deep financial expertise, a board will most likely have a director in their ranks with this type of advanced financial expertise; one who may have served as a CFO for a global corporation.

Some may argue that all board members understand broad-based risk management: a key attribute to a director's duties to be sure, and cyber security would simply follow these same risk management processes. But a key contributor in making risk-based decisions is analyzing the specifics of the identified risks, the likelihood of those risks, as well as the specific countermeasures in place to determine the potential impacts of a risk. If we agree on my very general definition of risk management, how can an effective risk-based decision be made if the specific risks, or specific countermeasures, are not completely understood? I am not inferring an understanding at the deepest level but a broad knowledge of cyber security: the threats and the basic risk mitigating measures that can be used.

Following the finance example, at least one board member could similarly have deep expertise in cyber security to help translate the details for other directors, who have broad-based risk management skills and a general understanding of cyber security. By understanding the specific cyber security context in the general risk management process, the risks and countermeasures can be better understood, resulting in better risk-based decisions. Because cyber security is so important for corporate success, I would advocate for increased cyber fluency across all of the board members, not just the identified member with cyber security expertise. Certainly I am not suggesting that each board member be an expert in security, however having the knowledge to question, understand the answers from the CISO, and the ability to advise based on this assessment, across the entire board, would be a key differentiator in corporate success. With your investment of time in reading this book, you are doing just that. The expert director could dive into more of the details, but with every director proficient in the basic, broad themes of cyber, it would allow them to discuss, challenge one another, and agree on specific cyber-related items.

2. The impacts of cyber security have increased exponentially in the past decade with increased risks, breaches, and regulations. I argue that the same level of risk velocity is not found in many other business domains, resulting in an increased need for cyber security expertise at the board level. Some may argue that adding a director to address each business domain specialty is not the best approach in building an effective board, and I somewhat agree. However, certain domains are more prevalent, impactful to the success of the company, and emerging at a high velocity (cyber security as an example), which require a more domain-specific specialty.

3. A management team and board may leverage consultancies, outside law firms, and advisory partners to assist them with understanding cyber security risks. These services have a cost associated with them, and if the risk velocity of cyber is so great and will require assistance regularly over time, these costs add up with each engagement. It may be more cost-effective to have a director with cyber expertise (as well as requisite business competencies) to replace many (not all) of these external engagements.

4. There were public comments to the proposed rules that reiterated the well-known fact that the cyber security industry has a shortage of experts. Even fewer are cyber experts who also have a deep understanding of business domains and could translate those skills to board service. Some commenters concluded that the proposed rule to require disclosure of board expertise should not be finalized due to this shortage of experts.

    As a CISO who builds security strategies and hires the appropriate staff to fulfill those services, I've never identified an important issue that needed addressing but decided not to address it because finding the appropriate talent would prove too difficult due to a lack of available resources. Instead, my team and I worked on innovative solutions to find the appropriate talent or build it. The limited talent pool is a separate issue from the core issue of the need to have cyber security expertise on the board to enhance risk-based decisions and oversight, an issue that should not deter a board from including such an expert director.

    If history has taught us anything, it is this: the days of government not being involved in the cyber security initiatives for companies have long passed. We will see more regulations in the future, and it is my belief that one of them will include a required disclosure of cyber expertise on publicly traded boards. I believe the SEC proposing the rule, but not finalizing it, is akin to a turn signal in our vehicles. The intent of the direction the industry is heading was made clear, even though it wasn't fully realized in the final rules at this time. Learning from this, companies should aggressively search *now* for cyber security experts who also have deep knowledge of business domains to serve on their board. This will ensure that your company isn't frantically searching for this type of director after disclosure becomes mandated and after all those companies who wait for regulations to address cyber security begin their search. The early bird gets the worm. Even if my belief is wrong and future regulations do not require disclosure of board cyber security expertise, what is the impact of proactively including such a director in the short term anyway? You will have addressed a growing risk for your company by strengthening your board with the expertise to critically evaluate your cyber security program.

Lastly, as an industry, programmatic changes in training, board certifications, and other innovative processes to better prepare future cyber security executives for board service cannot be understated.

For those companies that proactively seek to add to their board capabilities with a director who possesses cyber security expertise, there are some distinctions that should be considered. These distinctions could help ensure that the level of cyber capability is adequate, and if disclosure requirements do indeed surface in the future, any cyber security-specific expertise expectations will be met (in the eyes of both the regulatory entities and the investors).

Many boards have added directors to their ranks who possess expertise in IT due to the emergence of technology as a business enabler. Directors who have served as CIOs or chief technology officers (CTOs) for major corporations can translate the technical underpinnings of a digital strategy into business terms so that the board (or committee) can advise on these strategies. Recall from previous chapters that the role of the CISO has increasingly been organizationally separated from the CIO and IT organizations for many companies. There may be cases in which an experienced CIO independent director did not lead the cyber security function for a company because security reported into another executive's organization. In cases such as these, the technically fluent director may possibly lack deep cyber security expertise by not being directly involved in its oversight. And technology expertise is vastly different from cyber security expertise.

In other circumstances, a former CIO or CTO director may have indeed led a cyber security function with the CISO reporting directly to him or her. As a result, these CIOs are more aware of cyber security initiatives for the company but may still rely heavily on the CISO to guide them on cyber-related topics. The information security field has grown significantly with many different disciplines such as security operations, risk management, training/awareness, application security, OT security, IoT security, and a host of others. A CIO director maintaining expertise in these growing security areas, while supporting proficiency in emerging, non-security technology and digital domains (such as artificial intelligence), may prove too challenging. A specialized cyber expert is needed if boards are to adequately address cyber risk.

But what exactly is a board cyber expert? It depends on who you ask. Browse the Internet and there is no shortage of industry reports, surveys, and research on the current state of cyber security expertise at the board level. Some of these reports highlight that the overwhelming majority of boards lack cyber security expertise, while other research shows a majority of boards have at least one, sometimes more than one, board member with cyber security expertise. And other reports show varying numbers in the middle. Why such a discrepancy in the results? My belief is that there are a few contributors to the variances in the findings.

For example, many reports are generated by leveraging survey data, asking the subject of the study to self-evaluate expertise, which can lead to interpretation issues by the respondents of what true expertise may mean. Additionally, some of the reports interchange the words experience with expertise, both of which are vastly different from one another.

In my personal opinion, I would respectfully challenge some of the surveys that showed a majority of respondents claimed their board had at least one cyber security expert or more. Did the "expertise" equate to a more general *expertise* in digital and technology knowledge that I previously outlined, and with indirect *experience* in cyber? Or was the expertise truly steeped in focused, specialized *expertise* in the domain of cyber security?

Without diverting too much from our topic at hand, it does seem appropriate to investigate a bit more on this notion of expertise, to understand the different interpretations of expertise and to come to a general agreement on what constitutes expertise in a particular field. Even a technology executive, such as a CIO, who may have had management duties over cyber security, in addition to digital initiatives, infrastructure, network, and software development, this experience does not lend itself to being an *expert* in cyber security. Instead, exceptional expertise in a specific discipline is something that is garnered through deep experience, advanced training, and years of focused practice – *almost exclusively in that domain*. Moreover, a true expert moves beyond individual practice and shares their expertise more broadly through public speaking, publications, etc., *in that specific domain*, to have peers challenge and critically review their views.

I trust my primary care physician and understand that she has the education and years of practice necessary in dispensing medical services to enhance my overall health. Yet, if I were to need, for example, heart surgery, I would seek out a well-respected cardiologist to perform that surgery over my primary care physician. Why would I do this, I just said that my primary doctor graduated from medical school and has years of great experience in dispensing medical services? The reason, and I am almost certain that you would make a similar decision, is that a cardiologist has years of specialized training and practice focused almost exclusively on the human heart, a devoted skill that I would find more valuable in performing my surgery. Moreover, such an experienced cardiologist may have contributed publications to scholarly medical journals and provided keynote speeches at medical conferences – all focused on the *specific* domain of heart health to help advance the industry.

There could be varying conclusions as to what constitutes the specific merits of expertise; we've just examined two of these conclusions. One conclusion was from survey respondents who believe that one or more of their board members have cyber security expertise, and the other was my opinion that the expertise stated by the respondents may not meet the same type of rigorous requirements for expertise that I defined previously. So, who is correct? Actually, there is no correct view between the respondents and myself. Expertise is a personal view by the individual who makes a decision or perhaps is most affected by the expertise. What another person considers to be an expert is irrelevant to me when I decide who will perform my heart surgery – it is my choice on what I consider to be an expert.

Consider another example: During a legal trial, prosecutors and defense lawyers may call board-certified experts in a specific field; often each side will have their own expert to give testimony on the exact same piece of evidence. Even though the lawyers (and the experts themselves) provide substantial credentials to establish their expertise, ultimately the decision on which expert is considered more knowledgeable and believable falls on the judge or jury of that specific trial. In the case of cyber security expertise on a board, it doesn't matter who labels a board member as a cyber expert, the ultimate judgement of that expertise falls on one person: the investor.

This is precisely why our industry needs disclosure regulations for identifying the level of cyber security expertise across different corporate boards; it will provide the investor with the knowledge to make their own informed investing decisions. As future regulations emerge, and potential disclosures into what each company constitutes as cyber security board expertise surface for the investors and the public to critically evaluate, I anticipate similar studies in the future will show (overall) fewer affirmative responses of self-proclaimed cyber expertise in the boardroom – until such focused expertise that can be appraised is indeed added and can be justified.

Adding a cyber security expert to your board doesn't forfeit a seat away from a director who can contribute to other important business governance matters outside of cyber. A well-qualified board candidate to serve as a cyber security expert should have both cyber expertise and exceptional business qualifications. The two attributes are not mutually exclusive, difficult to find, yes, but not separate from one another. Remember our example of the cardiologist who has deep expertise in the human heart? That doesn't presuppose that the cardiologist can only contribute to the medical community on matters of heart health. They possess a holistic medical knowledge apart from the heart and can add value to a wide variety of medical topics. Moreover, many cardiologists, and other specialty surgeons, often serve on hospital boards and medical industry panels, contributing to business decisions. Your board cyber security expert can add value too, across wide-ranging business topics, not just cyber. There are few functions inside a corporation that has a better, more visible role to all that is going on across the company: Cyber security is one of those functions. Such visibility lends itself to more comprehensive decision-making on a number of business issues.

BOARD GOVERNANCE

What could a high-performing board governance model for cyber security look like? Much as is the theme of this book, because every corporation is different, each company will have its own view of what success looks like in governing the cyber security program. What follows are some general themes based on personal experience, with an eye to the SEC rules previously outlined in this chapter.

THE CISO

You have read about the role of the CISO in the early pages of this book and the importance of placing a well-qualified expert with extensive business competencies as your leader of the cyber security program. Hiring the right person for your corporation requires your significant input into the recruiting process. Whether it is the identified director with cyber security expertise, a committee chairperson, or a panel of board members, interviews with the final candidates should include at least one at the board level. Having knowledge and confidence in the expertise of the incumbent is critical. It is my belief that to garner that confidence, direct involvement in the selection of the person is required.

For those companies who have proactively included a CISO into their business, it is equally important to understand the CISO's expertise and background. Get to know your CISO; I can say from experience, they know your background, as well as the backgrounds of each of your peer directors. Researching board members provides the CISO with valuable insights that assist them with performing their board reporting duties. The same can be said for directors having direct knowledge of their CISO regarding their core competencies and experience.

Engage your CISO in other activities aside from the regular reporting they perform for you. Enlisting their services in new director onboarding or special projects helps to provide you with more time to partner with them. Increased collaboration between the CISO and the board members helps to develop trust, a key component in the relationship. Instruct your CISO to include you in incident response tabletop exercises or other activities that will put you in a position to watch the CISO perform and gauge how they carry out their duties, as well as providing you with key insights on the incident response capabilities for your company.

The ideal director–CISO relationship would be one in which the partnership extends beyond a meeting for fifteen minutes every quarter, to a relationship that is built on trust and one in which the CISO is looked upon as a trusted advisor for you.

CYBER SECURITY BOARD COMMITTEE STRUCTURE

It may not be feasible (or desired) in the short term to develop a dedicated cyber security committee within your board structure. Sure, there are some corporations who have proactively done so, with my belief that many more will follow. But your board conversations may conclude that it is not preferred for your board to accomplish this currently, or maybe ever. In the absence of such a dedicated committee, I do advocate for a committee structure that provides more time for cyber security to be discussed, questioned, challenged, and advised. Traditionally, cyber was discussed within the audit committee of the board, but as previously outlined, this committee is inundated with responsibilities that may dilute the time and focus on cyber security. If the committee times can be arranged to allow for more quality cyber conversations, the audit committee structure may still be an effective choice to discuss cyber security for some companies.

The use of a technology committee as part of the board structure has been adopted by many companies and can include oversight of the cyber security program, as well as general IT, digital, and other technology programs within your company. Focusing the committee structure in this way helps to provide more time to invest in actionable conversations, and as a result, deepen the content of the cyber security agenda.

A good goal for your regular cyber engagement at the board committee level could include:

- **Topic Depth**: Moving from general updates with some security metrics to a model where relevant cyber topics for the business can be explored in more depth and importantly discussed. Examples may include emerging technology and risks; strategic shifts in your business and their cyber security implications; current capabilities and any gaps in the security posture; discuss acceptable risk levels; and cyber industry news/updates.
- **Frequency**: A popular cadence for cyber security interaction with the committee is each quarter, four sessions each year. This tempo works well for regular touch points with your CISO. In some companies, the CISO may present just once or twice per year in person (or via video conferencing) and supply only written updates to your board

technology platform for the remaining quarters. In these situations, directors should consider increasing the in-person (or via video conferencing) frequency to stay abreast of the company's cyber security program with the ability to ask questions, rather than a one-way information flow. The length of the cyber security update on the committee agenda should allow for a detailed, actionable conversation. In my experience, I believe thirty minutes should be the absolute minimum time allotted for the update – driven by a strong agenda of topics by the CISO, with your input.

- **Attendee Expansion**: The committee that has specific oversight of the security program will undoubtedly have the most interaction with the CISO. Meeting four times per year, and at a deeper level to understand enough to advise on cyber matters, provides the CISO with a great opportunity to share important information. Consider making one of your four cyber security updates a full board update. This can be done at the beginning or end of your fiscal year to give a good annual review type of cyber update for all members of the board of directors. These annual review sessions are also great for bringing in guest speakers on cyber security for the full board to be briefed. Federal law enforcement, CEOs of cyber security companies, and industry experts can help elevate the discussion among your full board. Lastly, any board-level updates by the CISO related to a material cyber breach or significant incident should be provided to the full board of directors.

BOARD EXPERT ON CYBER SECURITY

Your potential board expert on cyber will have a unique relationship with the CISO, one that I suspect will be much different from most partnerships we've seen historically between security executives and the board. Capturing this opportunity would mean more in-depth conversations between the two in order to explore:

- How security strategies are being prioritized and executed.
  - With an understanding of each of the components in the cyber security strategy, the board cyber expert can unpack each one to ensure it is comprehensive, rightly prioritized, and cost-appropriate for the company. In recurring conversations, exploration of how each project is progressing, as well as positive and negative impacts to the business for each, will provide the director with solid updates.
- Ensuring that detection and response methods are adequate to maintain continuity of business.

- Investigating the specifics of how the security program monitors for threats, inclusive of people/process/technology, any gaps present, and extended conversations on the ability to provide strong incident response capabilities, is paramount for the cyber expert director so that guidance can be applied.
- Identifying any gaps in the security program and potential opportunities to remediate them.
  - Through direct questioning, the director with cyber expertise can inquire if the CISO has the resources needed to deploy and maintain an effective security program. Where gaps are present, assessing the root cause can be drawn out in these more in-depth discussions with the CISO so that guidance to management can be performed.
- Share threat intelligence related to the business.
  - This is a wonderful opportunity for the cyber expert director to talk with the CISO to better understand external threats related to the company's security program, or indirectly associated with it. Understanding the threat landscape specific to the company's industry, or perhaps even more targeted threat intelligence regarding the company itself, can provide very good insights. Exploring what other companies are doing in a particular domain and/or general cyber security hot topics can add value as well.
- Confirming that the people, process, and technology attributes of the security program are holistic, with strong integrations with the core business.
  - It is within these conversations where the director can get a feel for the security specifics of particular operating segments within the company. What does the security for any payment card processes look like? How robust is the security for the operational technology that drives manufacturing at the company? These discussions help to evaluate how the security organization links its initiatives with the business – a critical component of any security program.

It is my belief that in order to have such quality-oriented discussions, the frequency of board cyber expert/CISO should be more than once per quarter. Instead, a monthly cadence would allow for not only identifying subject matter capabilities/gaps but also monitoring progress to the execution of security strategies, as well as emerging threats and/or shifts in business strategies that require adjustments in the cyber security services delivered to the business.

When the committee or full board updates are provided by the CISO, the board cyber expert can provide commentary to the main themes and serve as a translator for the non-cyber experts on the board (particularly in

Potential Cyber Governance Model

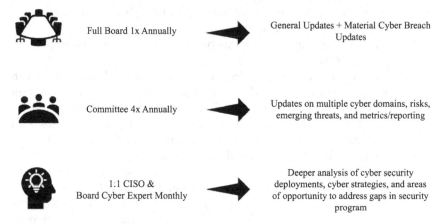

Figure 11.1 Potential cyber governance model.

situations outside of the board/committee security briefing, when the CISO is not present).

I can almost hear the collective voices from many of my readers: "This certainly is a significant amount of time to devote to cyber security for the board of directors, is this much really needed"? I agree that such a governance model (see Figure 11.1) does propose a significant amount of time, more so than we've seen in the past. However, considering the escalating significance of cyber security and its impact to the success and well-being of our companies, the investment and effort are minimal when put into perspective.

CYBER RISK OVERSIGHT

One of the rules from the SEC requires disclosure on a company's processes for identifying and managing cyber security risks and threats. Such disclosure would require a significant amount of awareness to these activities by the board, in order to deliver more than just a macro-level response to broad cyber security themes.

In my junior high school math class, our teacher's homework assignments comprised of working through various math problems and writing the final answers for her to grade. As we progressed in the year, we tackled more complex mathematical topics, including algebra. Sometime around the halfway point of the school year, as the work became more difficult, my teacher asked us something that many students dread to hear when it comes to homework: "I want you to show your work". The final answer was no longer enough; we had to show our work to demonstrate how we came to the final answer. Now both the answer and demonstrating our competency to achieve it were graded.

To me, the final SEC rules on disclosing details of the company's cyber security oversight equates to my eighth-grade math class so many years ago: *show your work*. It will no longer be enough to demonstrate cyber security competency at a macro level and that core elements exist at your company. We must now show more details of how we arrived at that macro level of security. I anticipate there will be significant dialogue on this disclosure rule, but ultimately, our responsibility will extend to providing much more details on our cyber security programs than ever before.

Without question, the final SEC rules will elevate the cyber security discussion at all levels of a company. Significant ongoing work is needed to be prepared for our disclosure requirements. While there is no magic formula for all companies to follow, the one common understanding will be that companies will need to devote substantial time, more than ever previously required, to enhance and/or demonstrate proper cyber security governance. The duty to preserve shareholder value extends beyond mere compliance to a security rule – it is also enhancing the cyber security posture for our companies to help maintain a continuity of business.

Notes

1 U.S. Securities and Exchange Commission. *Cybersecurity Risk Management, Strategy, Governance, and Incident Disclosure, SEC 17 CFR Parts 229, 232, 239, 240, and 249, Final Rule.* U.S. Securities and Exchange Commission, July 26, 2023.
2 U.S. Securities and Exchange Commission. *Cybersecurity Risk Management, Strategy, Governance, and Incident Disclosure, SEC 17 CFR Parts 229, 232, 239, 240, and 249, Final Rule.* U.S. Securities and Exchange Commission, July 26, 2023.
3 U.S. Securities and Exchange Commission. *Cybersecurity Risk Management, Strategy, Governance, and Incident Disclosure, SEC 17 CFR Parts 229, 232, 239, 240, and 249, Final Rule.* U.S. Securities and Exchange Commission, July 26, 2023.
4 U.S. Securities and Exchange Commission. *Cybersecurity Risk Management, Strategy, Governance, and Incident Disclosure, SEC 17 CFR Parts 229, 232, 239, 240, and 249, Final Rule.* U.S. Securities and Exchange Commission, July 26, 2023.

Section Two

Cyber security overview

The first half of this book focused on the industry, the role of the CISO, board engagements, financing security, the cyber security strategic plan, and execution of the plan, all of which are directly applicable to the development and ongoing operations of your corporate information security program. You may have discovered that many of the concepts we've explored so far in this book are not a large departure from baseline program consider-ations important to other business disciplines. Where the confusion sets in is around the technology surrounding cyber security.

What follows in Section Two is a more broad-based view of many cyber security topics that serves as an overview for directors who may have focused their careers on other important business disciplines, which requires them to better understand some fundamentals of cyber security. Even though it is a broad-based view, there are tips woven into the following topics that can be leveraged to probe more deeply into one's own cyber security program and should not be overlooked by directors who may have some cyber fluency.

Chapter 12

Security operations

Considered by many to be the lifeblood of a cyber security program, security operations (SECOPS) include the very technical components that seek out vulnerabilities and the threats that attempt to exploit them. In this chapter we will review several disciplines related to security operations, and while certainly not a complete roster of operational topics, the list provides a glimpse into some of the top areas in which you should understand at a high level in order to make meaningful guidance. For our purposes here, I don't mention vendor names or their branded technologies in this section, withholding these references only provides more focus on the core topics themselves.

DETECTION

It is no accident that I begin this chapter with detection; it is the primary function that I look for in an effective cyber security program. After all, a company cannot address threats that they don't know are coming at them. I would never diminish the need for preventative controls, but detection is the core capability that lends itself to effective response, which means faster times in getting back to business. To repeat a mantra mentioned in an earlier chapter, it isn't a matter of if, but when, and detection is the first step in addressing the incident.

We've discussed many options for building a detection capability, be it in-house or through an MSSP, as well as the multitude of technologies available for detecting threats. No matter the choices your company pursue, the most important factor is possessing a capability to consistently monitor the network every minute, every day/night, every year.

We'll explore the technology-based aspects of detection but supplementing them should be a robust and easy way for all employees to report incidents. "It takes a village" is a common saying that very much relates to security; creating and communicating a method to all users on how to report suspicious activity is paramount.

DOI: 10.1201/9781003477341-15

A key component to detection lies in endpoint protection technology that is deployed across endpoints including laptops, desktops, servers, mobile devices, cloud components, etc., to look for suspicious activity. Historically, security teams leveraged basic anti-virus (A/V) software that matched technical signatures of files and executables on the computer to a database of known malicious signatures. If they matched, the file was quarantined. While it provided some benefits, the negative aspect of this technology was that it was reactive, relying on the need to keep the signature database up to date to ensure what was found on the system could be matched to a known malicious signature in the database. Moreover, there are rapidly growing instances where a malicious exploit is widely available prior to a signature being developed.

The security industry responded with several different types of next-generation endpoint protection solutions. From sandboxing technology that "detonates" files, allowing the code to run in a safe environment to determine if the code is malicious or not, to Endpoint Detection and Response (EDR) and Extended Detection and Response (XDR) that pull in multiple sources of security data. These latest technologies help to separate critical alerts from those identified as nuisance or insignificant. Endpoint technology has matured significantly, and the industry is filled with very good products that can help remediate (not eliminate) threats.

By probing into the details of the endpoint protection deployment, you can better understand the level of detection provided and ensure there isn't a false sense of security merely because the company owns such a technology. How complete is the deployment? Is the endpoint protection technology deployed broadly across the company, or are there gaps in coverage? Is the technology locked down in such a way that makes it difficult for users to disable or remove the protection? Is the sensor technology updated to a recent version or is it leveraging an older instance? Does the protection work when the system is offline from the corporate network? These questions help to understand the level of protection afforded with the investment. The answers should reflect a comprehensive deployment of endpoint sensors that are up to date and are configured in such a way as to not permit end users from easily disabling (either accidently or purposely) the protection.

Another term that you may hear in your cyber discussions is SIEM (Security Information and Event Management), often pronounced "sim". In simplest terms, this technology ingests log and machine data from a large group of disparate origins such as network devices, security tools, infrastructure devices, applications, endpoints, and more. The purpose of the technology is to take all the information from these data sources, analyze it, and correlate it to identify potential issues, ideally before they become issues. The concept is that one log incident from one source may mean very little, and another log event from another source similarly may not trigger alarms, but together, these events could be an indicator of something more serious. Using a fraud example, the SIEM may identify that a consumer of your product or service edited their contact and address information, while another log source identifies a transaction from that same consumer less than twenty-four hours after the address change. This may equate to a legitimate event for the customer, but it could also mean that potential fraud may be taking shape and something the company may want to investigate.

The obvious goal for SIEM would be to ingest as many value-added logs as needed so that more complete analysis of the environment can be performed. But historically, SIEM solutions have been expensive, many charging by the amount of data brought into the system. For companies on a limited security budget, this could mean fewer logs are brought into the system, reducing the full value of the capability. SIEM vendors have responded with different pricing options that don't charge solely by data consumption, while at the same time other companies have been created to provide ways to optimize/cleanse the data prior to ingestion by the SIEM. You should explore with your CISO if there are any negative impacts to the effectiveness of the SIEM deployment as a result of the pricing model your company leverages. Your CISO should explain the pricing option that provides the most value, not the least cost, for the company's SIEM deployment and if that option lends itself to an effective security capability.

We often equate security technologies with the core mission of protecting the enterprise, when in fact these technologies can also assist other areas of IT, and potentially the business, for non-security-related tasks. They can provide another valuable data point for IT assets, operating system types, and other metrics, and can contribute to troubleshooting IT-related issues. For business, the solutions may aid in providing intelligence for business operations, digital deployments, and manufacturing processes. Unlocking the potential of a company's investment in security by including it in other business areas provides higher value and is something that should be explored when discussing detection and SIEM capabilities. Like with most purchases, leveraging enterprise pricing for larger orders unlocks larger discounts from the vendor. Evaluating how many teams can benefit from these technologies, even outside of the information security organization, identifies if the full value of the investment can be enjoyed, or if it is being used as a point solution for just one area of your business.

VULNERABILITY MANAGEMENT

Seeking out weaknesses in systems so they may be strengthened, thus reducing the window of opportunity for them to be exploited, is at the heart of vulnerability management. Enterprises use vulnerability scanning solutions to scour their IT environment to assess its assets for vulnerabilities. As with other security platforms, it is important for companies to ensure they have purchased adequate licensing from the vendor to be able to scan their entire infrastructure.

There are several industry vulnerability classification and reference methodologies, one example is the Common Vulnerabilities and Exposures (CVE) model. Each vulnerability is assigned a unique identifier to distinguish the vulnerability, as well as associated references to it, and is rated by severity using the Common Vulnerability Scoring System (CVSS).

Depending on the score, vulnerabilities are assigned a severity of low, medium, high, and critical, which allows the security operations and IT teams to focus on the most critical vulnerabilities first. Some teams may further identify and score vulnerabilities that relate to specific systems that support critical business processes. All this detail helps to provide an understanding of the security posture for the company regarding vulnerabilities in systems and applications.

Once vulnerabilities are discovered, the process to address them is called patching, which includes obtaining the patch or update, testing it, distribution to the affected systems/applications, and finally installing the fix. It is natural for IT teams to have a thorough, planned process for installing updates and patches. Another process is called hardening, which is similar to patching except hardening involves making configuration changes to systems/applications, so they are in a more secure state than before the hardening. During standard operations, these processes are important to keep the systems updated and occur on a recurring schedule. However, when a vulnerability is so severe, the IT team will patch or harden the environment on an accelerated schedule. You should inquire how this type of emergency patching process works for your company. Moreover, insight into how effective the patching process is via metrics like percentage of systems patched, and other measurements, will prove valuable in understanding the capabilities to respond to these emergency situations. Of particular interest should be the patching performance on the systems that drive the company's critical business processes. Worth noting is the patching metrics should be measured and published by an independent team, such as information security, rather than the group who does the patching (in many cases, a team in the IT organization). Having the team who performs the patching also be responsible for reporting on the effectiveness of the patching may introduce a separation of duties concern.

The steps taken to patch a corporate environment are extensive and include tasks such as testing, backup procedures, and deployment of the patch, to name a few. But one of the most significant areas in vulnerability and patch management lies in a proper inventory of corporate assets and the types of operating systems and applications in use at the company. This discipline is called asset management, and without a robust program to identify assets within the corporation, vulnerability management (and other security operation endeavors for that matter) will not be as effective as they should.

Searching for vulnerable systems and providing needed updates/fixes to them may not appear to be a cutting-edge security control, but this foundational process is critical to the hygiene (and security) of a corporate infrastructure. These vulnerabilities are what the adversary looks for in a corporate network. To accomplish a successful preventative program requires a strong partnership between the information security and IT teams within your corporation. In working together successfully, this multi-departmental program will be enhanced.

APPLICATION SECURITY

Whether a company develops its own code from a blend of frameworks, purchases commercial off the shelf (COTS) software, or customizes COTS software, ensuring that the code is secure as possible is critically important. If not addressed (preferably during the build and customization phases of development), software and coding vulnerabilities could lead to major problems for a corporation. The primary method for securing software lies in the software development lifecycle (SDLC) which aims to develop a structured process, through phases, to produce secure software for use in production. Security is very much a part of this important SDLC process to protect against insecure design and coding mistakes.

Providing security training to software developers serves as a great incubator for a successful development program. Discussing the many different coding mistakes that may lead to software vulnerabilities helps to demonstrate for the developer their role in secure software coding practices. It may prove effective to "gamify" the training to make it exciting for the participant developers and introduce competition in completing the training, so each developer strives to win over their peers.

You may hear your CISO mention something called a bug bounty program. Simply put, these are programs in which a company (usually those developing software) provides incentives for reporting software bugs (vulnerabilities) to the company. These incentives can be some form of recognition or even compensation of varying amounts.

Testing the software code can help identify issues and there are many security vendors that provide products and services to conduct this type of testing. Two common tests are static testing and dynamic testing. A static code review is done before and during the development of the software, evaluating the code and issuing a report. You may want to inquire about the impact for speed to market the software developed (or customized) by the team because of security testing. It may be the case that the overall static testing program takes quite a bit of time to perform and when reports are generated, several false positives may be presented. After researching the false positives and correcting the true vulnerabilities, typically another scan is done to verify coding fixes. All of this takes time and could impact how quickly the company can introduce new capabilities. Exploring how the application security program addresses these potential delays while maintaining the effective security of the software provides informative discussion topics for you and the CISO.

Dynamic testing involves testing when the code is executed and checks for the functionality, security, and performance of the software. This testing is done after the development phase and as a result, any fixes will most likely be more expensive to correct than fixes done during development.

All these components work together to provide a more secure application development program that aims to identify vulnerabilities early in the development stage. Through wrapping security into the overall SDLC process, enhancing developer training, and providing efficient testing for vulnerabilities, the application security program can be a beneficial addition to the cyber security program.

ARTIFICIAL INTELLIGENCE (AI) SECURITY

One of the most difficult days for an information security professional is the day after a technology company delivers a major product launch amid huge fanfare to the public. Inevitably it leads to employees asking their security teams if they can plug in their new, ultra-awesome consumer product into the corporate network. Usually these consumer devices are not designed for corporate use, and may not be safe for use in a business environment. Similarly, every once in a while, a new technical advancement emerges that sparks huge industry interest. The marketing firms get ahold of it, massive demand ensues, and soon security teams across the planet are being asked to secure a new technology in a very short timeframe.

If I wrote this book twenty years ago, I would be discussing the emergence of consumer mobile phones being used for business purposes. Had I written it seventeen or eighteen years ago, it would have been securing wireless networking technology. These emerging innovations have stabilized over time as more resources are invested to explore any risks and then develop subsequent security strategies to address them. But at first introduction, security teams scramble to understand how to best minimize risks associated with them, while the business is scrambling to exploit the benefits of the technology. I am including a section on AI here, as that is what is dominating the headlines at the time of this writing. Employees, industry peers, senior executives, and even board members are asking about AI; employees want to use it, and senior leaders want to know how we can leverage it in a secure way to reduce overhead costs to maximize profits.

It is still relatively early in the mainstream lifecycle of AI-related technologies, specifically generative AI, so information security teams require time to evaluate and search for associated risks and potential countermeasures to reduce those risks. To be sure, many organizations, including the U.S. Government, are also exploring how generative and other forms of AI will impact industry. For example, the U.S. President recently issued a Presidential directive that seeks to develop an AI strategy to guard against misinformation and other potential downsides of the technology.

Even with the need for more analysis, there are some things you can inquire about with your CISO regarding AI-related and AI-generative technologies while our collective security teams are performing their analysis. Ensuring that the security program keeps sight of the basics without a sole hyper focus on the technology is a good first start. In security, often what we should do is focus on the behaviors and not the technology. For example, a company may have historically had a policy that said no cameras are permitted in their data center. Over time, video camcorders became smaller and those were added to that policy to keep them out of the datacenters, as well. Then the emergence of mobile phones began, and more phone models included cameras. The policy would be expanded to include no cameras, no camcorders, and no mobile phones with cameras are permitted in the datacenter. In this particular example, the technology was the focus, losing sight of the behavior the company was trying to address: *no photographs are permitted inside the datacenter.* Our programs should put the attention on the behaviors we are trying to enforce (or disallow) and not solely focus on technologies that serve as a tool to these behaviors.

Additionally, focusing on the behaviors will drive more directed outcomes related to what we call the CIA triad (confidentiality, integrity, and availability). Companies could strive to ensure that confidential information is not put into public-type AI-generative technologies. Moreover, addressing the integrity of the data outputs from AI solutions, ensuring that the information is internally and externally consistent, should be top of mind. Leaders depend on data to make business decisions and making sure the integrity of the AI-generated data being used to consider those decisions is crucial. These safeguards are not unique to AI technologies and are no different from the managing the CIA within messaging applications, email, or other technologies in use by corporations. Stick to the basics and address the key concerns.

To convey expectations, it is wise for corporate security teams, in partnership with legal and privacy, to draft a policy directed toward generative AI usage to explain to employees what is allowed, and which actions are not permitted – as determined by the company.

Many technology providers are exploring new ways to integrate AI-related technologies into their suite of products. Office productivity solutions and many other applications/services in use today are expanding their offerings (or rapidly developing them) to include AI or generative AI type of technologies. Chasing each one of these technology deployments separately may seem futile. Perhaps the best path is to conduct security reviews of a few solutions that can be used as corporate standards which can provide employees with the ability to leverage AI types of technologies that have been reviewed by security. Aside from the security benefits, standardization of technology also helps with controlling overhead costs. Without clear guidance, corporate teams from all over the globe may leverage disparate technologies based on team preferences, which can drive up costs. Channeling users to a few specific technologies and documenting the few exceptions for non-standard use could help reduce the costs of leveraging a multitude of different technologies within your company. Additionally, it could reduce the costs associated with support departments such as procurement, legal, IT, corporate card expense reporting, and others in processing the purchases and installation of the disparate technologies. While standardization makes good sense for all technologies in your business, the overwhelming tide of excitement around generative AI makes standardizing even more critically important.

We are in a very early stage with AI-generative technology use for business: early from the security assessments of the different types of AI technologies, early in understanding the unintended and potential malicious uses of AI, and even early in the governmental legislative aspects of its use. Continued security research of AI, as well as sticking to the core protective strategies of cyber security, will ultimately help to stabilize this emerging technology, just as it did with mobile phones in business and wireless networking.

CLOUD SECURITY

It isn't an exaggeration to say that cloud computing has transformed the IT industry by introducing efficiencies in performance, cost, dependability, and many other categories. Like with any technological advancement, security concerns surface that need to be analyzed and addressed so a company can potentially enjoy the proposed benefits.

The cloud introduces a web of complexity both technically and administratively. Customers may leverage a blend of on-premises and cloud infrastructures and possibly use multiple different cloud environments from different cloud providers. There are public clouds, private clouds, and a host of services such as software-as-a-service, infrastructure-as-a-service, and platform-as-a-service. When adding in technical details such as virtual machines, hypervisors, containerization, and many more, understanding cloud computing in executive terms can prove challenging, particularly when making core business decisions.

Additionally, there are administrative complexities that make cloud computing, well, cloudy, when it comes to strategic business judgments. We explored in an earlier chapter the very detailed roles outlined between the cloud service providers and the customers, each one with specific duties as part of the relationship. Moreover, removing the infrastructure from company-operated datacenters and placing them in the hands of a cloud provider open new questions such as, "where does my data reside", "can I perform an assessment on the security of my provider", and other important questions.

Adversaries understand that these complexities can work on their behalf and have targeted many of their efforts on cloud infrastructures. They look for cloud misconfigurations by the customer, perhaps inadequate access controls, exposed storage areas, default passwords, all within an environment that may not have proper monitoring or logging controls. The proliferation of cloud, along with the increased complexity and security threats, is enough to confuse even the most cyber-savvy business executive. By exploring the main themes of security in the cloud with the CISO, you can better understand the business risks associated with its use. Areas to question may include:

1. Does our cloud infrastructure leverage a zero-trust type of model? This is to say that the company assumes every user of the environment, and every device may be a threat and requires robust authentication and constant validation.

2. What is our level of monitoring for our cloud environment(s)? There are offerings for monitoring that look at performance, cloud usage, and costs/fees associated with your cloud deployment. Equally important is security monitoring from a variety of security and cloud monitoring tools to look for malicious activity across all your cloud instances. In both cases of IT and security monitoring, it is important to have benchmarks in place that help to identify when a measured activity exceeds a pre-determined, appropriate threshold.

3. Do we have strong identity and access management (IAM) processes in place for our cloud environment(s)? Ensuing that access (by user, system, or other entity) is controlled, authenticated, and monitored is vital for today's new deteriorated network perimeter infrastructure.

4. What security tools do we have in place that protect our cloud environment(s)? Ensuring that these tools are present across all your various cloud instances (and providers) is critical to provide maximum coverage. Once this has been determined, the depth of the security tools is worthy of analysis. Already mentioned was adequate access control, and the security platform should address threats related to identity and authentication. Cloud services/applications consist of several different processes, databases, containers, and a host of other elements that make up workloads. Ensuring the security platform helps to protect these workloads can help in providing a better security posture.

5. Do we extend the capabilities of our standard internal security program to different environments, specifically in the cloud? You've

spent a significant amount of time in reviewing your company's security program, and ensuring that similar controls extend to the cloud is a great next step. Foundational items in your security program such as data classification and incident response should include how they are addressed in the cloud. The CISO will be able to explain what security services may require special consideration or potential changes to accommodate securing the cloud instance(s).

IDENTITY AND ACCESS MANAGEMENT

IAM is the discipline that encompasses technologies and processes to provide access to systems/applications for authorized entities. Many books on the topic of IAM alone have been published and to be sure, the discipline can get very detailed, very quickly. From simple topics such as passwords to complex federated IAM programs, there isn't a lack of content with regard to building a robust identity program. For our collective goal here, I'll only cover the basics and you may extend your knowledge through conversations with your CISO.

Just because a person may be an authorized employee of your corporation doesn't mean they require access to a system or to high levels of access within that system. Known as "least privileged" access, users of a system/application should only have the access to effectively perform their job – and nothing more. Even top executives and other employees who may even have U.S. government clearances still only require a need to access just the information to perform their duties. If authorized access is not used over the course of a pre-determined time, then that access should be revoked.

Username and passwords have been the primary first line of access control but over time, they have been found to be less than optimally effective. As an industry, we tried to enhance passwords by requiring longer character lengths, adding special characters, requiring regular changes, and not reusing past passwords. In turn, this has led to issues with users remembering their passwords or using the same password for multiple accounts (a very bad practice). There are products that store encrypted passwords so users can remember just one password and have strong passwords saved in the product for easy retrieval and use. Even with these enhancements, passwords remain as the primary, albeit less-than-optimal, method for authenticating an identity by leveraging something we know.

The emergence of multi-factor authentication (MFA) hoped to address password inefficiencies by requiring an additional step in the username/password authentication process. Through a text to the user's mobile device, or perhaps a code generated through a physical token, this step seeks to confirm that the person authenticating is actually the authorized person because they possess another factor besides something that they know – something they have. MFA introduced stronger capabilities for authentication but is not without risk. Several industry publications have explained that adversaries can potentially circumvent the MFA text process; if interested, your CISO is a good source to explain the findings of these reports.

Additionally, there are authentication applications that provide MFA by generating a random code. The user enters their username/password, and then the system requests the random MFA code. The user opens the authenticator app to obtain the code, then enters it into the desired system/application. Another option with authenticator apps is a quick option to confirm an access request. When the user enters their username and password into the system in which they desire access, the authenticator app presents an option to authenticate with a YES or a NO button. The user presses YES and the authentication is completed. While this MFA option is easy on the user, it comes with potential issues – one example is an MFA fatigue attack. Should an adversary obtain the stolen username and password of a person, they can attempt access to a system multiple times, generating several MFA authenticator app requests to the user. In some cases, a user may press YES due to the nuisance, or uncertainty, of the repeated requests.

Even with some of the risks outlined previously, MFA remains a strong preventative addition over just username/password authentication; your CISO can provide guidance on the best MFA type for your organization. The CISO will also keep you updated on the status of multi-factor deployments across your organization. I have been asked multiple times by senior leaders and board members, "Why can't we just turn on MFA for everything, right now, all at once, so we can reduce our authentication risk in the short term?" It seems a logical request but in doing so, it may introduce other types of issues such as operational risk.

Without testing and due diligence, one cannot anticipate all of the potential impacts to production that would be felt by implementing another step in the authentication process – particularly for system-based access. Additionally, does everyone in your organization possess a mobile device, or is willing to put a corporate application on their personal device? Moreover, are there potentially call center or manufacturing groups that require hard token MFA devices? Like with most things in cyber security, implementation requires a methodical process for testing prior to just flipping the switch.

In today's perimeter-less computing world, the importance of IAM takes on an important role. Previously, we operated with a model where the bad guys were thought to be on the outside and trusted employees were on the inside. Today, we must leverage a model where we should assume the bad guys are already on the inside and protect our systems accordingly with a zero-trust model. A robust IAM program is, in part, how we can achieve this.

The discipline of security operations extends to many other areas as well, but for the purposes of this book, what are stated above are adequate to understand the foundational operational controls for your company. Prior to engaging in discussions introduced by the CISO on areas such as threat intelligence, red teaming, ethical hacking, and the like, you should ensure the foundational controls mentioned previously are adequately addressed and functioning properly. Our adversaries follow the same model; they look for the easy vectors to launch their attacks, the open doors and windows of unpatched systems, etc., and because of this, it's where your security program should start.

Chapter 13

Incident response

Even with all the preventative controls, detection capabilities, administrative security controls such as policy management and security awareness, all combined in a layered security program, at some point your corporation will need to respond to an incident. Data breaches and threats are commonplace today, perhaps even in your personal life you may have experienced the nuisance of replacing a credit card due to a compromise of your information. This inevitability of incidents requires a formalized and practiced incident response plan that guides the enterprise in a structured way during the chaos of a breach.

What is an incident? Or better stated, which incidents rise to the level of critical severity that requires immediate and complete attention? Your CISO and team see millions of events pour out of the security platforms that have some sort of anomaly aspect to them. Looking at all of these events, one would think that every adversary across the world is trying to break into your corporate environment. Events are common, the majority of which end up being nuisance types of alerts, low severity concerns, false positives, or appropriate business processes that perhaps generated an event alert. After pruning through these events, much of which may be done with automation, perhaps a couple dozen remain that require further investigation. Of those, one or two *may* rise to the level of a serious security concern, possibly initiating the incident response plan process. Merely looking at the number of total events will not provide the data for your board to make actionable business decisions.

Traditionally, external auditors meet with the CISO each quarter to discuss the cyber security program with one inevitable question: "Are you aware of any security events or incidents that occurred during the period of performance (quarter)"? This used to be an easy question to answer with very little ambiguity. Today, however, as external firms increase their cyber security knowledge, more regulatory implications surface, the public awareness of cyber breaches grows, and the impacts to the cyber insurance market are felt, these external entities want to know more about all incidents impacting companies.

The intent of the question has remained the same over the years; they seek to understand impacts that are significant in nature. Perhaps a more applicable question to get to the spirit of the inquiry would be, "are you aware of any *material* security incidents that occurred during the period of performance"? But what is considered material? Some external firms may do a good job of dictating what materiality is when inquiring about an incident, but as our industry grows, defining the terms: event, incident, and alert, will remain a challenge.

Security platforms provide rich detail into network and system activity. Depending on the vendor and their product, the security professional can view alerts based on criticality of the alert, see how the potential threat traversed through the network or system, obtain information on the system such as operating system, user, etc., and perhaps even a geographical representation of where the alert is taking place. What security employees don't see is a skull and crossbones icon representing the adversary moving across the screen to make it easy to identify malicious behavior. In many cases, valid credentials are stolen and used to illegally access the network, so the security engineer only sees what appears to be a valid employee's actions.

As a board member and committee person, you may not find value in understanding, or even knowing, about the potentially millions of events that your security team is alerted to each quarter. Your interests lie in understanding those incidents that impact bottom-line efficiencies and/or top-line revenue growth; anything that hinders your ability to manufacture products, provide services, and transact with your customers. The best way to decipher the distinction between noise and material incidents is to create thresholds (in advance) for what types of incidents are brought to the board's attention.

Once a process is in place to provide actionable updates to the board, it is wise to give notice to how frequent the updates to leadership should be provided during an actual incident response. Too few updates result in uncertainty to the progress of the response, while too many may impact the responders' ability to effectively work on the response. In the wake of Hurricane Katrina, I was part of a small team that was charged with rebuilding a business segment located on the Mississippi Gulf Coast. All of us balanced the reconstruction of the corporate facilities with the rebuilding of our personal homes. As we worked on restoring IT services, it was important that we provided updates to our corporate office and the executives who desperately needed information on progress. We had generators running to provide power to the "war room" in which we all coordinated efforts. Fans were blowing consistently to provide some relief from the relentless southern Mississippi summer heat in buildings with no power. Large jugs of hand sanitizer were placed throughout the room for ensuring proper hygiene in an environment where mold and other airborne particles were of concern. Puddles of murky salt water were everywhere, and it was commonplace to see an occasional snake traversing through the building. Stress was high, we were uncomfortable, and working long hours.

Several times each day, we would leverage conference calling capabilities that we fashioned together to provide updates to the corporate office up north, 1002 miles away. We found ourselves spending more time in providing these updates than actually working on the core mission of restoring services. After some compromise, we found a balance that allowed us to make progress on the restoration while providing the needed updates to management.

As a matter of fact, most of the major incidents I have been part of in my career have always started with several updates per day in the early phases of the response. After realizing that there wasn't much new information being provided with each new update, management realized that there was a need to balance updates with the time it takes for response, and subsequently reduced the update meetings to twice per day, rather than one per hour. All responses are different, and some may have more workstreams than what other responses may require. Through an understanding for the need for customized updates dependent upon the response type, a pre-determined update and communication plan is a good process to have ready.

THE RIGHT RESPONSE

Not all incidents are created equal and each one may require a more nuanced type of response. For example, we explored earlier that adversaries may have different tactics and motivations. Adversaries who are loud in their attacks, such as hacktivists, may launch denial of service attacks or deface websites. Their noisy tactics require an immediate and complete type of response. Nation-state threat actors may operate under stealth, not wanting to raise alarms so that they can quietly occupy victim networks for extended periods of time. Responding to this adversary in the same immediate way as a hacktivist will alert them that you are aware of their presence. They will just fold up tents and move to another portion of your network, possibly forcing the security team to find them all over again. In this case, knee-jerk reactions can cause more harm than good. While incident response follows repeatable processes and best practices, you should inquire of your security executive about any variations in response when it comes to different types of attacks from different adversarial types.

EXTERNAL SUPPORT

Everyone requires assistance from time to time and incident response is no different. During extreme times of chaos and confusion, having a trusted partner who can assist you with the response will provide much needed piece of mind. The most effective way to prepare for a worst-case cyber event is to have a pre-paid incident response retainer with your preferred partner – in advance of needing the service. It provides you with the opportunity to pre-negotiate the bank of hours desired, the hourly cost of those hours, and service level agreements with the partner. These retainers are typically good for one year and if your company doesn't leverage the retainer for a cyber event, the pre-paid hours can often be used for a host of other partner services such as table-top exercises, security staff training, review of your corporate incident response plan, and many other specialized services. It is strongly recommended that your CISO and executive team lean toward pre-paid retainers rather than just an agreement on which partner the company will call in case of an incident. In doing so, your company reduces the risk of a partner not having the resources to react at the time of your incident, or the ability for the partner to charge elevated costs for response services when you need those services the most.

As important as the pre-paid retainer decision is with your incident response program, understanding which partner your CISO chooses is critical as well. There is a high likelihood that your company will leverage third parties such as outside counsel and cyber insurance providers, particularly if the response is being done under privilege from your law department. When choosing an incident response partner, it is imperative that the CISO checks with outside counsel and the insurance provider to ensure that your cyber security partner is on their desired or approved list of security providers. For example, if the determination is made to bring in an externally preferred cyber firm that worked previously with these external entities but is not your company's cyber response firm, time delays may be introduced. One of the first things the new security firm will want to do is deploy their own sensors on the global network systems to understand what is happening on the network. The installation of these sensors takes time even under the best of circumstances, and I have seen deployment times lasting two weeks during an incident. In a critical security incident, two weeks is a lifetime, time you don't have when answers are needed quickly. Having an approved partner, particularly one who leverages your currently deployed sensors, allows the cyber firm to quickly begin assessing the situation utilizing your already installed technology rather than installing new sensors.

If the response is to be done under privilege, it is prudent to have discussions with outside counsel, the cyber security partner, and internal teams to talk about the flow of response information. Due to its privileged nature, in many cases the cyber firm will only work with outside counsel who is leading the privileged response. Once the response is complete, the external law firm may dictate the type of format for the final report: a fully detailed written report, a written executive summary, or a conference call to discuss the findings. Pre-response discussions will ensure that all stakeholders have access to the appropriate information during the response while protecting the privileged nature of it. Your internal general counsel and outside counsel are great resources to consult with on the appropriate path for how the company responses under privilege.

THE INCIDENT RESPONSE PLAN

During the fog of an incident, response steps could be missed or perhaps all the needed stakeholders are not included. To prevent situations like these and to ensure an effective, repeatable process for responding to breaches, an incident response plan is developed, communicated, and practiced. While there are many components to an incident response plan, the core elements for your company's plan may include:

- Reporting and compliance requirements
- Roles and responsibilities of the various stakeholders of the incident response team
- Communication plan
- Incident handling procedures

An effective response is a team effort. It is imperative to identify all stakeholders who can bring their expertise to the response process so that all facets of the response can be professionally addressed. It is natural to include the obvious members of the response team such as the CISO, information security team, various teams from the IT department, legal, and executives. Equally crucial is the inclusion of representatives from public relations, investor relations, finance, communications, facilities, human resources, and others. Additionally, there are external members of the response team: outside counsel, external PR firms, cyber security partners, and others. The goal is to identify all stakeholders and outline the incident response roles and responsibilities for each. Beyond this, it is imperative that all members of the response team fully *understand* their roles and the expectations of their contributions to the overall response.

When the team has been identified, establishing the method for communicating effectively is an important part of the plan. Who will be responsible for external reporting? Who updates the executive team and board of directors? Who alerts the insurance company in a timely fashion to adhere to the reporting requirements? How often does the response team meet to provide updates? All these considerations should be planned in advance so that multiple communication workstreams can be successfully accomplished simultaneously. Additionally, there may be situations in which internal communication mechanisms (email, etc.) may be potentially compromised or brought down by the adversaries, requiring an "out of band" communication platform for responders to share information. Planning for this in advance can help to ensure the integrity of the communications is sustained.

The incident handling procedures incorporate many different elements and provides the team with a detailed guide on important tasks. While many of the steps are intuitive by nature, especially for cyber security professionals, pre-assembling the procedures helps to reduce the risk of missing or incomplete steps during a high stress response environment. Moreover, the procedures provide a validated approach for incident response. They are effective and they work. Commercial airline pilots leverage years of experience in aviation to deliver their passengers safely to their destinations. Even with all this experience, they still rely on pre-flight checklists to ensure all steps have been completed. While the overwhelming majority of flights do not result in an incident, following the pre-flight checklist with vocal validation of the completion of each step by the cockpit crew is a good system to ensure flight safety. Similarly, pre-designed response checklists lend themselves to highly effective cyber responses.

Cyber security professionals are an eccentric bunch. They love nothing more than to dive into a complex issue or dissect a technology to see what it can do, versus what it was designed to do. These are the folks we want on our side when things go sideways during a breach. I recommend a task for your incident response plan for when a breach is first discovered that runs counter to this enthusiasm from your team – send several of these energetic employees home immediately.

Once the team begins working on the breach, the energy level is high, but after about twelve hours, the team is fatigued and may not operate at optimal levels. If the entire team is working on the response, at that twelve-hour mark, your entire response team will slow down considerably. By sending a large amount of your responders home immediately to rest and spend time with their families, when the current team begins to tire, you have a fresh bench of cyber professionals to step in and continue the response while the initial team goes home to rest and re-energize. It is also a good idea to use geography as a response enabler. If log analysis or a similar investigatory task is required, assigning that to cyber security professionals on your team halfway across the world ensures that analysis is being worked while the local team is resting. Demand management and resource allocation should definitely be part of your response plan to safeguard against a weary team.

The incident response procedures should include a financial component as well. At the end of the response, a natural (and needed) question to ask your CFO is "how much did the response to this breach cost us"? With so many employees from various departments inside and outside the company involved, figuring out how many labor hours were used can be difficult without a pre-determined method for tracking response hours. It is wise to develop a cost code or other hourly tracking mechanism with your finance department that all stakeholders can use to track their response time during an incident. In doing so, after-incident reports can be generated on the hours involved, as well attributing them to the specific hourly rates for the individuals. There may be other mechanisms that can supplement the internal tracking, billable hours to an external law firm or public relations agency, for example.

Post breach conversations with partners, customers, and external entities can become unwieldy if no plan exists. After a response to a breach early in my career, the company averaged four to five requests per month from external partners to discuss the attack and any controls being implemented to reduce the risk of future attacks. For many of the large partners, we would fly to their home office to meet with their teams in all day sessions, conveying the state of cyber security for our company. Other engagements included conference calls or questionnaires looking for specifics of the incident. These interactions were vital in assuring our partners and other third parties that appropriate measures were being taken; however, they also impacted the cyber security resources of our team. Ensuring your company is ready to address these inquiries through a detailed process involving a cross-functional team of experts in cyber, communication, and business operations is of the utmost importance to manage concerns, as well as resources.

RANSOMWARE RESPONSE

With the increased prevalence of ransomware attacks, a popular boardroom debate has grown over recent years on the topic of paying, or not paying, a ransom demand from an adversary who has encrypted the company's systems, possibly rendering them ineffective in normal business operations. This debate remains active without a definitive answer in the industry on what a company should specifically do or not do. The response to a ransomware attack will fall under the company's incident response plan, with all the considerations outlined in this chapter remaining relevant to this type of incident. Yet, there are nuances to the response that seem essential for this type of attack, which we'll discuss in this section. It is important to understand that ransom decisions are unique to each company so what follows are thoughts from my experiences, as well as witnessing what some companies and the industry have experienced. Any of the following opinions on addressing ransomware are my own; go forward strategies for your company can only be attained after thorough internal discussions.

The person who decides on whether to pay or not pay a ransom should be outlined in the incident response plan, preferably at the executive level, with clear documentation that identifies the company's decision-making authority (and perhaps a back-up person should the primary person is unavailable). The CISO, general counsel, CIO, COO, and other functional executives advise the decision maker on potential impacts and suggestions, but the ultimate choice is made by the decision maker, potentially the CEO or other senior executive, with input from the board of directors.

There are several things to consider when deciding to pay a ransom. First and foremost, interactions with cyber criminals in and of itself should be weighed. The person or team that breached your network and caused disruption have already exhibited behaviors in conflict with appropriate business transactions. Moreover, they have attempted to extort money (Bitcoin, etc.) from your company to unlock the systems. These behaviors do not point to a high degree of confidence that future dealings with them will be forthright and professional. If the ransom is paid, there is no guarantee that systems will be unlocked by the adversary, that the decryption process works completely, or that they will not disclose your proprietary data anyway. Additionally, once the ransomware attack is successful, there are no guarantees that the same person or team won't attack your company again, demanding another ransom.

I've enjoyed fishing since my grandfather first took me as a young boy, and any time I get an opportunity, I like going out on the water to relax and try to catch my daily quota. I normally don't fish in areas I haven't tried too many times in the past. I always go to the sections of the lake or ocean where I have consistently caught fish before – I know that area has a better chance of success because it has worked for me in the past. Similarly, if the adversary has seen previous success in breaching a specific network and was paid, it stands to reason that the likelihood of future attacks and payment success for them on the same network may be better than average. When a ransom is paid, there is no promise by the adversary that they won't attack you again.

There are companies that specialize in negotiations between the attacker and the victim company. For a fee, these companies negotiate attacker's demands to lower the ransom amount and serve as an intermediary between the two. While the negotiating firm may be reputable, the "breach supply chain" of the victim company, negotiator, and attacker still includes one non-reputable entity: the attacker. Even with just one bad player in the chain, the overall process still includes the potential for unreliable conclusions, even with the other two reputable companies are performing ethically.

While no preventative controls work one hundred percent of the time, an argument can be made for a strategy that allocates funding in appropriate back-up systems and ransomware protections in a thoughtful budget process over time (before a ransomware attack) rather than spending millions on ransoms, only to have to implement security controls anyway at a later, post ransom point in time. A purely analytical, alternative argument may be that if I pay $2 million in a ransom, and it takes $4 million or more to proactively strengthen preventative controls, it makes sense to just pay the ransom rather than spending a larger amount on prevention. Obviously, this is a short-sighted way to think about this issue. It may appear that, in this example, paying the ransom is more cost-efficient than the time, effort, and cost to deploy preventative controls. But this argument only applies to this one instance. Imagine if it happens two or three times in a corporation, soon one would recognize that it isn't a viable alternative. Not to mention the impact to the corporate brand because of multiple incidents as a result of inadequate preventative controls. As such, these types of alternative risk mitigations should not even be considered.

All these deliberations should be discussed among your team and policies put in place prior to a ransomware event. Doing so puts all the decision-making processes on your terms rather than in an emergency when trying to beat a ransom demand countdown clock.

TURNING POLICY INTO PRACTICE

You've invested significant work in building out the incident response policy, honed its processes, and identified the roles and responsibilities for all stakeholders. You even identified situations in which slight nuances to the response plan may be needed. In the end, you have a well-thought-out plan of attack for an incident. But if it only lives in a document that is rarely looked at, the response won't be as effective as it could be.

Like with most things, a good repeatable process takes practice.

For every goal in a hockey game, behind it were several hours of ice time in the team's practice facility. Weight training, viewing game highlights, endurance training, and practicing plays, all culminated in the few seconds it took to score a goal. Imagine if a team did no preliminary work and only took the ice during game time, the results would assuredly show ineffectiveness.

A popular method for practicing your incident response plan is through table-top exercises. An attack scenario is created and introduced to your response team so that discussions and a walk-through of how the company would respond can be conducted. This is the time when mistakes and questions provide the most value. The more we learn in this environment, the better position we'll be in when the real thing occurs. In the Marine Corps we used to say the more we sweat in peacetime, the less we may bleed in war.

Leveraging a third-party partner to facilitate the table-top exercises can provide real value to your response practice. As mentioned previously, companies can leverage their cyber security partner for these services as part of their incident response retainer. A reputable firm will have a good understanding of the various attacks used, preferred vectors of attack, and some knowledge on tactics used. When engaging the partner, the CISO can help to describe what risks are most prevalent and the most important business risks the company wants to avoid. This helps to customize the table-top exercise to make it more realistic for the participants.

In building the scenario, different "injects" can be added to the exercise. For example, after the response team learns the main scenario (a ransomware attack at a manufacturing facility, for example) and begins working through the practice response, the partner will, at various intervals, add injects such as:

- News of the breach is beginning to hit the press outlets.
- The company's stock price has just dropped significantly because of the news.
- A reporter from a major news organization is on the phone and wants a comment on the breach.

These injects serve to disrupt the flow of the response and cause distractions, events that could possibly occur during a real-life scenario. Customizing the tabletops and providing injects make the training optimally effective. An important factor to consider is to ensure the scenario is not shared with the participants in advance of the table-top exercise. Our adversaries don't warn us about what they are about to do, so we should practice without participants' advanced knowledge, making it as realistic as possible.

Your CISO may suggest multiple table-top exercises: one for executives only, that serves as an awareness opportunity that shows what can potentially take place during an actual event; another for the technical teams to nail down the technical specifics of a response; and another for the entire response team in a full exercise.

During an actual event, there will be external parties assisting you in your response and recovery. Your tabletops should include these important external partners to make the response as realistic as it would be in a real incident.

In combination with an effective detection capability, an optimal incident response program ensures that threats can be identified quickly, and response processes initiated expediently, increasing the chances of the company returning to normal business processes quickly.

Chapter 14

Security awareness

In the mid-1970s, my family visited NASA's Kennedy Space Center in Florida as part of my childhood summer vacation. I was filled with excitement as I entered the gift shop after a day of touring the facility. On one of the shelves was a toy model of the lunar excursion module (LEM) used in the Apollo moon landings and I remember thinking there could be nothing cooler than to have one of these models to play with back at home – I had to have one. But, even as a child, I knew that achieving this goal would prove difficult.

My family didn't have much disposable income during my childhood and this vacation surely obliterated any we did have. If I went to my mother with the request, she would give me a thousand reasons why I didn't need the LEM model, so going through her was not a viable option. Another vector I could use was my father, but I knew his probable response would be to go ask my mother. My maternal grandparents were on the trip with us, perhaps I could leverage them? No, my grandmother was even more frugal than my mother and probably served as the role model for my mother's disdain for frivolous purchases. I approached my grandfather, a kind man who valued hard work, and told him if he would buy me the five-dollar LEM model, I would wash his car for him once every week for one month when we returned home. My strategy worked, I had chosen the path of least resistance, gave my grandfather something enticing for his efforts, and now I had a shiny new lunar module to play with on the ride home to Ohio.

Similarly, our adversaries understand that corporations purchase and deploy millions of dollars in security technologies and labor to reduce the risk of cyber breaches. Wouldn't it be easier to just choose the path of least resistance to gain access to the targeted network? In many cases, that least resistant path is our employees, and the vector is quite often, phishing – sending fraudulent emails enticing them to click on a link or download an attachment causing malware to be downloaded to their system. Or even worse is a non-malware phishing approach of tricking the employee by sending them to a fraudulent web page to input their corporate network

DOI: 10.1201/9781003477341-17

credentials, providing the adversary with valid login credentials. Variants of these types of attacks can extend to text messaging, impersonating an employee in a call to the help desk, and other technological avenues, making them a dangerous part of a user's workday. These attacks are popular because they work. Each day, users fall victim to social engineering attacks and one of the best ways to reduce the likelihood of a successful one lies in the discipline of security awareness.

Historically, security awareness was made up of compliance-type training modules, most frequently a ten-to-fifteen-minute computer-based training module, (CBT) that was required for every employee. Usually done at the end of the year and bundled with several other compliance training modules from other departments and disciplines, this type of awareness (only) did not provide optimal retention of the content. How can we expect that our employees will retain one fifteen-minute CBT module throughout the year?

Like with many things in cyber security, our industry evolved and began providing other types of awareness activities to enhance the ways our employees consume content. Though not an exhaustive list, what follow are some general areas in which security awareness has been enhanced.

AWARENESS ARTICLES

Throughout the year, timely articles on a variety of security topics can help to enhance cyber fluency across the workforce. Additionally, these regular updates can also be used to help our employees in their personal lives, away from work, by offering solid tips on how to protect themselves (and their families) online. The articles can be delivered through the corporate email system, or perhaps on the company's Intranet homepage, for employees to read when they have an opportunity.

Topics could include the dangers of phishing, risks associated with using unfamiliar USB thumb drives, or protecting themselves from online theft when shopping on their favorite website. It is important for the CISO and their team to develop a calendar of cyber security awareness articles that highlights when the article will be published during the year, the content/topic, and other details. In doing so, it is easier to build an awareness article program in which the topics build off one another. Additionally, the timing of the articles can be pre-determined so that messages are delivered at the optimal time. For example, a security awareness article highlighting how the employee can protect themselves while shopping online may be best delivered in the month of November, as the holiday shopping season begins to kick off in full swing. Doing the same article in the early part of the new year may not have the same impact than when it is needed most.

It is critical that the information security team works closely with the corporate communications department to ensure the articles are arranged in the corporate format appropriately, as well as ensuring the timing of the article is optimal. In many cases, the corporate communications team will limit the distribution of content that employees will receive from all the various departments so as not to overload the individual. Aligning on the schedule and content of the awareness articles ahead of time with the communications team will reduce the risk of last-minute shifts of when the articles will be delivered.

Lastly, there may be occurrences when a notice to employees is critical and requires immediate distribution. In partnership with the communications department, having a pre-designed process for emergency distribution of security awareness articles or alerts will help prevent delays in communicating to employees in a timely manner.

ROLE-BASED SECURITY TRAINING

Security is everyone's responsibility and certainly all employees can be a viable target for cyber criminals. However, there are some roles that rise to the top of the list of the most targeted individuals. Adversaries leverage online resources such as corporate websites, social media, videos, and other online tools to learn who holds key roles in an organization. Moreover, they can garner very specific information about a person, their likes, attendance at conferences, and more, to customize their social engineering attacks. CISOs should target security training for specific job roles that may hold more privileged access or availability to more sensitive data than other employees. These roles may include network and system administrators, corporate executives, and administrative assistants with access to those executives' email accounts, to name a few.

At the same time I write this, the industry is witnessing a few major corporate breaches as a result of social engineering. Specifically, adversaries are calling into corporate help desks/service desks to trick the employee by impersonating an authorized user requesting access to the corporate network. This is a good example of where role-based training would be effective by providing the help desk employees with examples of social engineering and the importance of following established rules for providing access to users.

The intent of role-based training is not to repeat the general security training geared for all end users; instead, it is to expand on the standard content to include specialized topics that are relevant for the job role audience attending the session. Specific threats, as well as attack types seen in the industry, are good additions to the training. By conducting this specialized training via an instructor-led training session, attendees can ask questions and engage in meaningful conversation on the content and how it relates to their role.

BROWN BAG SESSIONS

I have found success with adding brown bag sessions to the information security awareness program to provide employees with an informal, learn as you wish type of service. I am always fascinated by the level of employee interest in these sessions, which almost always includes a full conference room or large number of virtual attendees. People want to learn more about cyber security and how they can protect themselves (and their families) from online threats. This program adds one more training avenue for individuals to accomplish that.

The brown bag program could involve a reserved conference room, or video conferencing meeting space, typically during the lunch hour when employees can bring their lunch and listen to an informative session on a cyber security topic. At least twice per year, we will bring in food for attendees to enjoy as they learn. It is an informal, fun way to learn more about cyber security.

CYBER SECURITY AWARENESS MONTH

Each year, October is recognized as cyber security awareness month, a chance for companies to highlight the importance of cyber security throughout the month. Capitalizing on this opportunity requires advanced planning early in the year to create a program filled with activities and learning sessions that invite employees to learn more about information security in a fun way. What follows are some tips on what my teams and I have created during National Cyber Security Awareness month.

Promoting the awareness month starts in September with email blasts, posters, and a calendar of events that will take place in October. The goal is to generate excitement about the month-long event and provide employees with the chance to reserve time on their calendars to attend some of the upcoming activities. Pre-planning also involves administrative tasks such as booking conference rooms, reserving tables and chairs in common areas of the office to set up learning stations, as well as ordering any food or beverages for the events throughout the month's activities. Additionally, during the pre-planning phase, arrangements can be made with security vendors to provide give-away items for employees such as t-shirts, pens, webcam covers, and other small items.

On the first business day of October, a group of information security employees gather at the employee lobby entrance where tables are set up. Posters highlighting different cyber security topics adorn the walls of the lobby and tables are filled with cupcakes, wrapped in packaging with a note highlighting the internal website that details of the month's activities. This type of welcoming event helps to kick off the awareness month and get employees enthusiastic about the upcoming events.

The types of events a company can provide throughout the month are only limited by the team's imagination. Some examples of past events my teams and I have created are:

- **Password Strength**: Computers or tablets are set up in common areas for employees to stop by and enter in a password they consider to be strong. The application provides results of how fast the password can be compromised, the weaker the password the faster it can be compromised. Employees enjoy this activity because it is a hands-on way for seeing how well they can choose strong passwords.
- **Breach Notification**: A table staged centrally in corporate office's common areas, perhaps the cafeteria, has computers on them for employees to enter in their phone number and/or email address. The application will notify them if their email or phone were involved in a previous cyber breach.
- **Word Jumbles/Games**: At the beginning of the month, employees can pick up a packet with different games such as crossword puzzles, word jumbles, etc., that relate to cyber security topics. Throughout the month, the employees work on the puzzles and turn them in for a chance to win prizes.

An important consideration to make for those companies with multiple locations is to ensure that the awareness month activities take place across the various sites around the world, each one with as much fanfare as the corporate office. This ensures that some employees are not left out of the activities and reinforces that cyber security is a global initiative for the company.

National Cyber Security Awareness month is a fantastic way to focus on the importance of cyber security in fun and imaginative ways that employees enjoy. With some thoughtful, preliminary planning, your awareness month program can be successful in meeting these goals.

CYBER SECURITY BRANDING

Marketing the cyber security program can take many forms, one of the most effective ways I have found is to provide branded materials for the employees. The first step is to create a cyber security logo, and with the help of the company's digital and marketing teams, I have found wonderful results in developing a cyber security "brand" for the company. I typically don't like to create a logo from scratch or one that is vastly different from the corporate brand. Usually, I just leverage the official corporate logo with the name of the team, i.e., cyber security, information security, information security and Compliance, or whatever the organization's name, under that logo.

By using the corporate brand, it makes the approval process by corporate marketing a bit simpler, not to mention it highlights the already established brand for the company. I have steered clear of unique and special logos that are a departure from the official company marketing materials, and definitely without stereotypical images such as hackers with hoodies or similar references.

Once the security brand logo has been established, my team and I work to create, order, and purchase a wide variety of products with the new security logo embossed on them. We traditionally have two tiers of products: Tier One are small items such as water bottles, mugs, hats, pens, golf balls, etc., and Tier Two are more expensive products (coveted by employees) such as fleece pull-overs, polo shirts, backpacks, and the like.

Tier-One merchandise is good for small giveaways at corporate cyber security events, such as the cyber security awareness month activities mentioned previously. Tier-Two items are perfect for raffles, handing out to participants of table-top exercises and special giveaways.

In every company I have been a part of, this merchandise was highly desired by the employees and helped to strengthen the culture of security at the company. Employees talk to one another about how they obtained the item, which can lead to more in-depth conversations about cyber security.

CYBER SECURITY OPEN HOUSE

Every cyber security program is a part of the business, an enabler to keeping business processes functioning effectively, with the ability to recover quickly after incidents. Historically, cyber security was seen as a super-secret society that operated in the dark recesses of a corporation, but as the topic has gained significant attention, more people are curious as to what the security teams are doing to help protect the company. Additionally, they are interested in how they can assist in the mission, as well as how they can protect themselves from cyber threats. Many corporations have seen the need to bring cyber security to the forefront of business operations, recognizing that it is time for security teams to turn on the lights and emerge from behind locked doors to share their capabilities. A great method to accomplish this is through an annual cyber security open house.

As a standalone event, or as part of the National Cyber Security Awareness month in October, the Open House aims to share all the initiatives that the information security organization performs each day to help protect the corporation. My teams and I have put together many of these Open House programs during my career and each one is met with high enthusiasm from the employees.

Usually once per year, tables are set up in a corporate office common area or large conference room. The tables make up several stations, each one equipped with a computer and large monitor facing the center of the room. Behind each table is one or two members of the information security team and several small giveaways are displayed on the table for employees to grab. Each station represents a specific function or service that the security team provides; stations can be devoted to endpoint protection, vulnerability management, security awareness, policy management, forensics, and so on. At the specific station for endpoint protection, that technology is showcased on the display and the information security team members can explain what it does, what they look for, and how they react to certain threats. Similarly, the vulnerability management technology is displayed with commentary from the security staff on the type of tasks they do to find and address vulnerabilities. It isn't uncommon to have eight to ten different stations for an Open House, each one providing a glimpse into a specific service, and combined, how they all work together to protect the company.

Employees can browse each station at their own pace, viewing the technologies, asking questions, and learning more about the information security program. Tea, coffee, cookies, or other snacks are provided to make it an informal but informative event. In my career, these sessions alone have transformed how information security is viewed, sending a clear message that cyber security is a part of the business, not a secret standalone organization.

DYNAMIC AWARENESS: INTERNAL PHISHING CAMPAIGNS

When I was a young boy in rural Ohio, my mother always told me not to touch the stovetop because it was hot. In my young mind I had a notion that touching the stovetop would be a negative experience, but it wasn't until I actually touched it one Sunday morning that I realized why she warned me. It became personal to me. Through this empirical knowledge, I more effectively learned not to touch the stovetop. So powerful was this lesson, I remember it today, decades later.

Security is personal too; it is a state of mind that we have and is quite embedded in our nature. For example, if we hear of an uptick in violent crime halfway across the world, we are certainly sympathetic to the affected people and hope that the perpetrators responsible for the violence are quickly brought to justice. But if that same increase in violent crime occurs one block away from our own homes, we go on alert much more than when we hear about it occurring so far away. It became personal to us.

Security awareness training can often be looked upon in the abstract, with employees understanding that phishing attacks happen in the world, but the awareness activities are not personal to the employee. How can we make the training about the dangers of phishing more impactful to the end user? One answer lies in dynamic security awareness activities such as phishing our own employees.

Leveraging available technologies in the security market, security teams can create phony email phishing campaigns that try to entice the employee to click on a link, download an attachment, or enter their network credentials into a counterfeit website. If the employee should react to the internal phish by performing one of these actions, they are taken to a website that alerts them that everything is okay, this was just a test, they should not have clicked on the link and why, how they could have spotted it was a phishing email, and how to properly report future suspicious emails.

Powerful metrics are available for these phishing campaigns which can identify phishing test failures by user, team, geographic region, Internet browser, and many more dissections of the data results. Like many other data sources, it is best to look at trends over time rather than just one internal phishing campaign. Many variables are present that could skew the results for just one campaign. For example, one specific campaign may have been more complex and difficult to spot than the previous campaign. Or maybe there are things going on in the business that may lead to a higher click rate. For example, many years ago I approved an internal phishing campaign that persuaded users to click on a link to restore their password to a specific collaboration technology. The campaign was to be delivered to our end users the following week. I can't remember the details of if it slipped my mind or if I just didn't make the connection, but that same week the IT department migrated to a new collaboration technology – the exact same technology the phishing campaign referenced. As one can imagine, the click rate for that campaign was much higher than previous ones.

The phishing program within your company should start with basic, easy to spot phishing emails and transition to more complex ones throughout the year. Also important for global corporations is to alternate campaigns that have English-based phishing emails, with emails that are translated to the specific language of the various regions. By providing variety in your phishing program, the effectiveness of the training is enhanced.

An important aspect of internal phishing is doing something with the results. Rather than just reporting that a certain number of users have clicked two or more times in one year's worth of phishing campaigns, it is better to provide enhanced training for those users. Through mandatory phishing CBT training for these users, it provides them with a more detailed view into the dangers of phishing, how to spot them, and what they should do when receiving one.

I have heard from peer CISOs in the industry on the many ways they provide enforcement for end users who consistently click on phishing campaigns. There are several enforcement types that start with additional training, and some others that include disciplinary action. It is up to each company's leadership team, advised by the CISO, on what their company will do with users who regularly click on phishing campaigns, as well as how prevalent multiple "clickers" are at the company. In the end, the process is geared toward making our user community more aware of the dangers of phishing, and not to punish individuals. Each company must determine on their own how they go about achieving that awareness.

Lastly, there is discussion among some in the security industry that internal phishing is not the best way to train employees on phishing. Proponents of this view explain that the company may appear to be tricking their employees that the process seeks to find fault in our trusted employees. I don't agree. During my undergraduate degree in philosophy, we had to read very old philosophical texts (many of which were translated to English from another language), understand the view of the philosopher, form our own view on the topic, and write succinctly about our view, and any conflicts in opinion of that view with the original author. Our professor realized this was a difficult task for students and instructed us to exchange our final papers with one another, provide feedback, make changes to the original paper, then submit it for grading. I would get my draft paper back from my peers and the students wrote, "nice job," "great work," "this is awesome," and so on. When they received their papers back from me, the pages were covered in red ink with instructions to make this point clearer, lead with this argument, delete this point, and similar feedback. They were shocked and many asked me if I was mad at them, why am I being mean by providing all these comments about their work? I explained that I wasn't being mean, I was trying to help them to get a better grade. The "great job" comments I received do little to make my paper better. In the end, by helping our employees to be better shows them that leadership cares about their success. My view is that helping employees to be better at preventing phishing attacks shows them that we care, not only about protecting the company but also about protecting them at work and at home.

A well-designed internal phishing program is a great way to move from static types of training to dynamic awareness that make it personal for the employee. In my years of leading internal phishing programs, the overwhelming majority of employees enjoy the challenge of trying to spot the emails and enjoy the process very much.

Security awareness is a critical part of an information security program. Adversaries lean toward targeting people simply because it works. Attacking the person is one of the most common vectors for criminals to gain access to a corporate network. As such, developing a robust information security training and awareness program is vital for corporations.

Chapter 15

Policy management

While it may not be the most exciting aspect of cyber security, the information security policy program is the foundation for setting user expectations with regard to protecting the corporation and as such is a critical part of an information security program. The policies mandate what is permissible and what is not when it comes to computing practices for the corporation. It is important to understand that policies are created to provide direction to the users of a company's computing systems, and as such, the policies should be easy to understand and written with the end user in mind.

As a high-level overview, a policy program consists of the following types of documentation. Some organizations may include other documentation such as work instructions or topical manuals, depending on their needs. But the typical documents include:

- **Policy**: A high-level document, ideally one or two pages, which outlines general expectations related to a particular security topic. Policies are mandatory; every user must adhere to the policy. Policies are reviewed annually, and a good, high-level policy will require little edits during the annual review process because of the generality of the document.
- **Procedures**: Another mandatory document "procedures" expands on the policies and adds much more detail on expectations related to a specific security topic, which could include process steps, configuration requirements, or other considerations that apply to the policy.
- **Standards**: Also mandatory, standards provide detailed requirements related to the policy and perhaps technology standards for adhering to the policy.
- **Guidelines**: These are not mandatory and as the name suggests provide guidelines that are flexible for the user in implementation related to policies, as long as they adhere to the standards and procedures. As a point of interest for global corporations, there may be confusion regarding the word "guidelines" due to cultural interpretations. For example, in my career I have found that the term "guideline" is looked

DOI: 10.1201/9781003477341-18

upon as a mandatory requirement in certain country cultures, whereas in the United States, guidelines are recommendations. To some of these cultures, the word guideline is interchangeable with the word policy and are mandated. Should a similar issue arise for your global organization, this conflict in the expectation for guidelines should be addressed by the CISO to ensure everyone understands which policy documents are mandatory and which are recommendations.

Together, these documents make up the information security policy program for a corporation. They provide a reference for employees to understand the company's expectations of them when leveraging computing attributes and handling data. It is imperative then that every policy document is not filled with technical jargon that they don't understand. Of course, in some of the deeper, more detailed procedures, there is a need for technical configuration requirements and the like, but policies in general should be easy to understand.

When I arrived at three previous companies as the new CISO, I found that each security organization incorporated all aspects of the policy program: policies, procedures, standards, and guidelines, in one large document. Often times, this collective information security policy was over one hundred pages. I made cyber security my career and have a deep passion for it, but I even have difficulty reading hundred plus pages of security policy – how can we expect our employees to read it and understand it?

I have found success with the method that many companies employ in their policy programs. Policies are developed as one or two pages of very broad language specific to a security topic, i.e., data protection policy. It is a quick reference that gives the statement of policy, language regarding who the policy applies to, and other important information. Because it is high level, employees may want to know more details on expectations. To provide that detail, each policy is linked to other separate policy documents such as procedures, standards, and guidelines, all interconnected so the employee can read as much detail as they wish, without having to sift through a hundred plus page document.

Another issue with a combined, all-in-one document is that the document seeks to cover all information security topics. As a result, the document may not include all of the important procedural details related to every security policy. In the end, the program is left with trying to encompass too much, and at a cost of not covering each theme in enough detail.

It is imperative that the policy documents are stored in an area where employees can readily access them, typically on a corporate web page that houses other important policies. Perhaps your company leverages an enterprise governance, risk, and compliance (eGRC) platform that automates the approval process and stores the policies as well. Whichever method is chosen, it is important to store the policies in one location, if possible.

Residing in more than one area adds administrative overhead to ensure the policies are consistent between them and any changes made to one policy document should be made across all versions stored in multiple areas.

There may be instances where a particular employee or team understands the policy, wants to comply with it, but is unable due to extenuating circumstances. To accommodate situations such as these, a documented (or automated with logging) exception process is established, which gives the requestor time (if approved) to become compliant with the policy. These exceptions should be temporary in nature and not renewed continuously. Much like a temporary tire for your automobile, providing a provisional solution until you can get the tire repaired or replaced, it is not designed to be left on the vehicle. In the same way, policy waivers/exceptions are not to be granted as a long-term solution.

While not an actual policy document, another useful written report can be an Information Security Annual Report. Published at the end of the year, the annual report highlights the accomplishments of the cyber security program, applicable metrics, and a short- and long-term look into the coming year.

Policies are a critical component to an information security program. It outlines the expectations for employees regarding cyber security and conveys the overarching policy requirements as decided upon by senior leadership and carried out by the information security program. Ensuring your CISO has a well-established policy program that contains easy to read policies will help in supporting a culture of security that is needed in any corporation.

Chapter 16

Risk management

The concept of risk management is certainly not absent from the work you perform as a director for a company. To be sure, you are actively engaged in multiple types of business risk, whether it be regulatory, financial, supply chain, or a host of others. There is no shortage of potential risks that emerge every year; we have recently seen variable levels of risks associated with the pandemic, wars, and economic uncertainty that impacted the risk universe for many companies. To keep track of these fluctuating risks and their potential impacts, corporations have leveraged enterprise risk management (ERM) programs.

For each and every company that I have been a part of, cyber security, or specifically a cyber breach at the company, has been either the number one or number two identified risk on the prioritized ERM inventory of risks. At this stage in this book, you have a good grasp of the many different risks associated with cyber security, the work that your security team (and other employees) are doing to protect the company, and the potential impacts of a cyber breach. It makes good sense then that security is top of mind for the ERM program.

Involvement in the ERM process by the CISO can vary widely, some an active participant in the recurring meetings with executives, while others may just update cyber security content for the materials used by others in the ERM meetings. It is my belief that if a risk is so prevalent among ERM groups across companies spanning multiple industries, and that risk is considered so high as to rate in the top five risks for the company, it makes good sense to have the CISO as part of the ERM meetings and discussions. Besides the ability to talk about the general risk of cyber breaches for a company, the CISO can explain the details of contributing risks that feed into those general concerns.

Highlighting the downstream risks and how a corporation addresses them provides more details that speak to the likelihood of the macro cyber risks outlined in the ERM process. Usually done through what is called a risk register, the CISO and team outline all of the risks associated with cyber security for the company. Examples could include the inconsistent management of privileged accounts, or perhaps inadequate network segmentation to limit the level of access to sensitive data.

The risk register is not a one and done activity; it requires constant attention because, as you have read throughout this book, risks and threats evolve based on numerous internal and external factors. A shift in business strategy could significantly swing the risk posture of the company. As such, the risk register work is worthy of frequent nurturing.

There are many good platforms to conduct and maintain a risk register program. Due to its dynamic nature, such platforms are better at outlining risks than static spreadsheets that live on one or two employees' computer systems. Automation provides up-to-date information with workflows built in to allow for multiple people to develop and provide oversight over the risk program.

A multitude of risk frameworks, 9 and 12 box approaches, and other standard risk tools are available. Exploring each one is not a goal of this book, rather, it is just worth noting that whichever methodology is chosen, it should be standardized across your company so that everyone is speaking the same risk vernacular and with the same goals in mind.

Once all of the risk data mentioned thus far in this chapter are collected, the executives can begin to have a discussion and make decisions. After all, that is the goal of a risk management program, not to eliminate risks one hundred percent but to drive decisions on how a company addresses those threats through acceptance, transfer, or mitigation.

THIRD-PARTY RISK

We rely on partners, suppliers, and service providers to help optimize our businesses; each one contributing to our success by providing important capabilities, leaving us to focus on our core business. In many cases, we leverage their technology offerings or have network connections into their infrastructures so that real-time data and services can be delivered. Yet, along with these important partnerships comes risk.

Adversaries target service providers with this in mind, hoping that a breach of a partner can lead to lateral movement to its clients. It is important that the third parties we leverage have strong security programs which can help reduce easy opportunities for adversaries to be successful in their attacks. The difficulty is that third-party partners operate their own security programs, without oversight from your security organization. So how can companies protect themselves from the secondary effects of a partner cyber event? Many CISOs have built security services which seek to evaluate the security posture of a partner to determine any risks associated with conducting business with them.

The first component of a good third-party risk program, like so many other programs within cyber security, lies in good asset management. Identifying all of the third-party partnerships via a complete inventory of providers is the first important step. You cannot measure and assess risk for unknown partnerships. In many cases, the IT organization will understand many of the business relationships through the integration services they provide. But increasingly common are partnerships that do not go through IT and are referred to as "shadow IT". Perhaps a partnership was completed by a specific line of business, functional area, or a geographical region of the company; these partnerships are more difficult for the CISO to inventory. This struggle is often reduced through building internal relationships, perhaps through a BISO or cyber risk partner that was previously discussed in this book, to understand strategies across the various business entities. When there is still ambiguity for all the external relationships across the company, I've found success in a simple mantra: follow the money. At some point, through some channel, there may be evidence of the costs associated with leveraging a partner. Working with finance, I look to identify any service costs linked with external entities that my team and I are unfamiliar with.

Whatever process is used, the inventory should be as complete as possible and incorporate all types of partnerships. Often, we may focus on obvious major partnerships with Fortune 100 technology corporations or service providers, but the list should include seemingly benign types of engagements as well. Things like manufacturing equipment suppliers, maintenance services, robotics, heating/ventilation/air conditioning providers, and other types of engagements may not immediately come to mind as one that would introduce risk into our company. Any network connection or partnership could be a potential vector for attack.

When a new partnership is being considered, a popular process for evaluating third parties is through a vendor risk assessment. Questionnaires may be used to collect specific types of security information from the vendor, along with any formal documentation the vendor may share (i.e., SOC 2 reports that specify how they manage customer data, etc.). Some security teams may use different questionnaires based on the type of engagement that the company is considering with the partner. Vendors who do not deliver core or connected services may be given an ultralight questionnaire that covers only the basics because the likelihood of risk in doing business with them may be lower. At the opposite end of the scale, a scale that could include several intermediate levels, are those vendors who are deeply integrated into your company's infrastructure and/or can access consumer or other sensitive data. The potential for risk is much higher for doing business with these types of engagements and as a result require an extensive questionnaire. These questionnaires are sent to the vendor, preferably through an automated system rather than attachments going back and forth, and after completion the vendor returns the questionnaire for a risk assessment.

Security companies have emerged in the past decade to assist teams with evaluating vendor risk. Their technology looks for issues in a potential vendor's Internet-facing systems and operations to help feed a vendor risk score. In combination with your CISO's internal vendor risk review processes, more data are available for your security team to perform a more complete assessment.

Hopefully during the course of this book, you have picked up on the recurring theme that security is not a project-oriented, "one and done" type of activity. Cyber security requires constant nurturing – the third-party risk assessment process is no exception. Consider this example. Your CIO is interested in performing a review of the company's systems and processes that manage user permissions and access to network resources. A consultancy is selected, and the two companies agree that the consultant will perform a two-week assessment of the systems/processes and deliver a final report to the CIO on their findings. The consultant will not have access to these systems; their work is strictly done through interviewing the IT employees responsible for those systems. The consultant will ask about ongoing maintenance of the systems, how they are accessed, and the processes used to make changes within the system.

The security team performs a lower-level risk assessment due to the third party not having access to systems or sensitive data. It is determined that the risk in doing business with the vendor is low, they are approved, and they begin their work. Two weeks later, the work is completed, a report generated, and the consultancy delivers a presentation and final report to the CIO. The findings show that there is considerable work to do in order to enhance the company's systems and processes for managing user permissions. The CIO thanks them for the report, and in passing, the consultant shares that if there is interest, another team within their consultancy has a service offering to help correct and enhance these systems and processes.

The CIO indeed wants to leverage this different service and approves the work. No vendor risk assessment is completed because the same vendor has already gone through that risk process. The work begins and the consultants gain access to the systems and begins to provide enhancements to them.

In this example, the scope of the initial work the consultancy performed is vastly different from the hands-on services of the new statement of work. The new scope is riding off of the vendor risk assessment that was previously done when the risk was lower. A new vendor risk assessment should have been done due to this significant change in the relationship because the risk is much higher. It is important for the director to understand the details of the third-party risk management process through conversations with the CISO, ensuring that the scope of relationships is regularly reviewed to understand if changes have been made.

Businesses operate in a dynamic environment, full of technical, societal, supply chain, and consumer behavioral risks (to name just a few) that can affect a corporation's success. Risk management is a key administrative security control to help identify, track, and produce actionable insights to help executives make informed risk-based decisions. Because cyber security ranks highly on the corporate inventory of risks, developing and maintaining a robust risk management program is imperative for companies so that they can navigate through this dynamic environment.

Chapter 17

The path ahead

Thank you for your time in reading this book to explore cyber security and how it can be beneficial for board members to dive more deeply into the underpinnings of their company's cyber program. Your commitment demonstrates a spark in the evolution of cyber security governance at the boardroom level that is needed and, with a bit of work, can be realized. Board by board, director by director, increased dialogue on information security in the boardroom will intensify the top-down support for this critical business issue.

Setting aside any regulatory mandates, exploring cyber security and how your company can enhance the security program makes very good business sense. Notwithstanding the risk mitigating benefits of a good cyber security program, it can enhance the *quality* of your business processes as well. Yes, outdated systems can introduce security vulnerabilities, but by refreshing those systems to current versions, it could mean less downtime and enhanced performance of the machines that are driving your core business.

Employees who have administrative rights on their computers and are able to download and execute files from the Internet do indeed introduce security risks to your company. But consider the time and labor cost involved in re-configuring computers and correcting configuration errors made by non-IT employees by having those administrative rights. Realizing this means that in addition to the benefits of enhanced security, there may also be excessive labor cost savings.

Developing approved standards for the types of technology your company uses each day helps to reduce complexity, ensure that the technology footprint is controlled, and each standard is critically reviewed by the security team. But it also helps to limit the number of costly disparate technology implementations from various business units and geographic regions, which equates to cost savings. For example, if your approved corporate standard for a collaboration platform is clearly communicated, why incur the costs of adding multiple investments in other, non-standard collaboration tools

DOI: 10.1201/9781003477341-20

across the corporation, only because a particular team prefers a different platform?

These three non-security examples, along with many more, show that security can help to enhance the quality of your IT hygiene, as well as control some of your bottom-line operational costs, making your company more agile and profitable. Sounds like a business issue to me.

There are indeed regulatory mandates that seek to provide guard rails for corporations to deploy an effective cyber security program. Fines, negative publicity, and shifting attention away from a security focus to solely remediating audit items are something that every company wants to avoid. This book has detailed many topics that can assist you in ensuring your security program is proactive in nature, rather than relying on a reactive posture to regulations and external pressures.

Whatever the drivers, I am energized about the notion of further integrating cyber into the standard business conversations already being held at the boardroom level. That is the primary aim of this book: to suggest an environment in which the CISO and board members can work together on a more regular basis so you can evaluate, question, challenge, and advise on how your cyber security program can help increase operational efficiencies and address cyber risks.

Achieving this goal doesn't require that you become an expert in cyber security; you have so much to be concerned about when it comes to advising your corporate executives on other important business matters as well. Instead, your role could be to work with your fellow board members to create a platform, an environment, in which cyber security issues can be more frequently discussed. And in those discussions, your ability to understand the general themes of cyber will assist you in your advisement duties. My hope is that this book provided you with the general understanding to do just that.

Developing more regular discussions doesn't mean devoting an exorbitant amount of boardroom time to cyber security. Much like a security budget, large increases in the cyber budget aren't necessarily the answer – it is the value derived from those investments that we do make which matter. The communication environment that you create should be enough that you and your peer directors can provide informed guidance, and as a result, increase the value of those discussions.

Advancements in technology, as well as growing partnerships with third parties, have deteriorated the corporate network perimeter. Adversary capabilities have grown significantly with a long-continued motive of theft and disruption. Increased regulations, large cyber insurance rates, and breaches becoming more commonplace than unique, all have contributed to cyber security becoming a recurring topic among corporate leaders. All against a backdrop of a security industry that has seen a shortage in qualified expertise to meet the demand, and ambiguity into the role of the CISO as a business executive.

More than ever, cyber security needs more corporate attention to transition it from "the shortest hour" of the year to something that is dynamic and frequently discussed. You've taken an important initial step by reading this book. I look forward to what you will achieve in helping to transform the way that cyber security is addressed at the board level.

Appendix

Cyber security inquiry checklist

CISO role	Recruitment	Does the CISO job description generate demand for applicants who are business-oriented technology executives, or do they highlight deep technical requirements that are mis-aligned with the CISO role?
		How involved is the board of directors, a subset of the board, committee, or individual director in interviewing final candidates for the CISO role?
		Ensure your final candidates possess very strong competencies in finance, strategy, accounting, human resources, and operations.
		Evaluate the overall CISO tenure at previous employers for final candidates, looking for experience with executing a cyber security strategy, rather than just creating a strategy.
		Explore, through the use of scenarios, how final candidates approach risk management, looking for discussions on likelihood of risks in addition to severity and impact.
		Gauge final candidates (through examples) on emotional intelligence and the ability to stay calm in high stress situations.
		Look for ways that candidates can explain technical concepts in easy-to-understand ways.

(Continued)

	Organizational	Review which executive role the CISO reports to, ensuring it promotes the importance of cyber security to the company, and provides unfiltered access to executives and the board to report cyber risks.
Compliance	Structure	Evaluate if cyber security is looked upon merely as a compliance topic in your organization; advise on any appropriate changes needed.
		Are security initiatives looked upon as a project or audit item that can be checked off as completed; how are security issues treated versus audit issues; advise on any appropriate changes needed.
	Cost of compliance	Evaluate the labor demand for your cyber security professionals to conduct audit type activities in your company. Analyze if the cost of cyber resources to address any audit items is sufficient or can more cost-effective labor resources be used to manage audit-related tasks.
Current board interactions for cyber security	Structure	Do cyber security updates to the full board occur regularly?
		Do cyber security updates to a committee occur on a regular basis?
		Does the CISO perform the updates to the board/committee?
		Which committee is responsible for the oversight of the cyber security program? Technology Committee, Audit Committee, Cyber Security Committee, other?
		Are each of the updates conducted in person/virtually or are they provided solely in board documentation?
	Frequency	How frequent are the information security updates to the full board?
		How frequent are the information security updates to the committee?

	Content	What is the average amount of time allotted for each of the cyber security updates on the agendas?
		Are the security updates consistently addressing large scale, programmatic changes to the security program?
		Do the metrics provided focus on risk, emerging threats, internally biased data, and actionable metrics? Or are they focused on number of alerts, number of vulnerabilities, and other similar types of data?
	Other CISO engagements	Is your CISO involved in other board engagements besides regular updates? For example, new director security orientation, 1:1 interactions with committee chairperson, special projects, etc.?
Information security assessment	CISO assessment	Was the information security assessment interview based or did it include technical assessments such as compromise assessments, penetration testing, etc.?
		Did the assessment leverage internal reports such as external and internal audit reports, other security assessments, etc.?
		Was the assessment benchmarked against an industry framework such as NIST, ISO, or CIS controls?
Cyber security strategic plan	People	Does the security plan source the entire labor request with highly qualified candidates with several years of experience (which may be unrealistic)?
		How does the strategic plan address the lack of industry candidates with significant cyber experience?
		Are there training considerations for security staff in the strategic planning?

(Continued)

Does the strategic plan outline the current skill sets of the security team and detail the critical skills needed?

Are single points of failure and remediation of them a part of the strategic plan?

Is there a plan for standardizing security job roles?

Are security leaders focused on supporting employees or do they provide individual contributor type of tasks?

Docs the strategy include unique job roles such as chief of staff, deputy CISO, etc., and explains the value of each role to assess if these types of roles are needed?

Process

How frequently is the CISO engaged with the business, touring facilities, and offices, to understand business needs?

Is the strategy aligned to common security frameworks such as NIST, ISO, and CIS controls?

What sources fed into the strategic planning? Peer insight, research firms, etc.?

Does the strategy focus on foundational practices such as vulnerability management, etc., or does it include highly sophisticated cyber security processes such as threat hunting, intelligence, etc. (foundational items should be fully addressed prior to moving to sophisticated processes)?

Does the company have an information security governance committee that is comprised of senior leaders who regularly discuss cyber topics?

Is the security program centralized to a shared service or are there disparate security functions each providing security services within the company?

	Technology	How does the company address, if applicable, leveraging a security partner that bundles all capabilities into one vendor offering to minimize having "all eggs in one basket" if/when an outage occurs?
		Is there a comprehensive methodology that address professional services to ensure that once completed, the internal team can address updates and configurations without having to pay a vendor to provide these updates?
	Strategy approval and publishing	Is the strategic plan presented in such a way to allow for easy decision-making among the management team?
		Is the strategic plan widely presented to various groups within the company to share information, garner feedback, and anticipate execution risks?
Strategy execution	Risk acceptance	Does the company leverage risk acceptance or risk transfer forms?
	Execution organization	Is the execution of the strategy tracked in a formal platform, identifying workstreams, tasks, and updates?
		Are the execution workstreams reviewed regularly in meetings to identify what is on target, what schedules are at risk, etc.?
Financing cyber security	Budgeting	Is there an incremental budget strategy that funds cyber security over time rather than sporadically after incidents?
		Does the budget plan contain fiscal consciousness to the company rather than just advancing the cyber security program?

(Continued)

	Measurements	Do the ratios used to benchmark cyber security spend align with the global organization rather than just IT? Note: cyber security often services areas of the business not serviced or organizationally aligned with the IT organization.
		Are multiple budget metrics used to identify industry trends over time or do they measure a single point in time that may not be relevant to your organization?
		Is the security budget looked upon as a project, a one and done type of investment followed by a flat budget in subsequent years? Or is the cyber security budget reflective of business decisions, evolving threats, and ongoing changes to the enterprise?
		Do the security budget metrics focus on external data such as industry average to brand impact as a result of a breach, data loss costs, etc. or are more valuable internal metrics used for measurements?
	Budget requests	Do justifications for budget accurately calculate cost savings, if any, i.e., labor cost savings, etc.?
		Are the budget areas for security prioritized based on criticality, risk, and likelihood of risk?
		Are there considerations to the timing of budget requests, identifying when each expense will hit the budget in the fiscal year?
		Is there analysis of capitalization vs. operating expense for all budget requests?
Role of security vendors and consultants	Vendor relationship	Is the inventory of security service suppliers and vendors categorized by impact to the organization: strategic partner, vendors, etc.?

	Vendor selection	Does the selection of vendors include analysis of desired attributes for a product/service by the CISO?
		Does the selection of a vendor satisfy a majority of desired attributes or focus on just one attribute, i.e., pricing?
		Does the outsourcing of services provide high value or merely addresses the servicing of one security technology. Is there a value analysis performed to compare insourcing vs. outsourcing a particular capability?
	Outsource decision	When considering building an internal capability, i.e., monitoring, are all costs examined to determine true cost: facility costs, labor costs, technology costs?
		When considering leveraging an MSSP, what are the desired qualifications and selection criteria used to ensure the MSSP has a high quality of service?
		Is there a cost analysis performed for all insourcing/outsourcing decisions, i.e., labor costs per hour for internal employees vs. consultants and service providers?
		Does the decision consider insourcing some challenging work to help retain experienced talent rather than paying highly qualified staff for simple monitoring tasks?
Security service management	Service catalog	Does the security organization use a service management structure, or are services provided on an ad hoc basis, as needed?
		Is there a documented organizational structure to the different service towers within security, identifying buckets of like services?

(Continued)

		Within each bucket, are there discrete services identified?
		Does each service have a service catalog document that provided service description, SLOs, reliant services, cost of service, how to order the service, etc.?
	Operations management	Is there a program to document the operations of the security program, or are the operations accomplished using disparate processes across the security team?
		Is there a documented program to identify all of the security technologies used, details of the technology, vendor information, and topical manuals?
		Are documentation requests, i.e., cyber insurance, regulatory, etc., completed individually for each engagement or does the security program leverage a database of responses to ensure accuracy and provide a one-to-many type of completion?
Future cyber security governance at board level	SEC regulations	Request a complete overview from the CISO and chief legal officer/general counsel on your company's strategy for compliance to the SEC rules.
		How will the company determine materiality of a cyber-related incident?
		Are the new reporting requirements included as a process step in the company's incident response plan to ensure the four days after materiality notice is achieved?
		How will the company report on their processes for assessing, identifying, and managing material risks from cyber security threats, as well as the material effects or reasonably likely material effects of risks from cyber security threats?

What is the plan for describing the board of directors' oversight of risks from cyber security threats?

What is the plan for describing management's role and expertise in assessing and managing material risks from cyber security threats?

Are there governance processes, committees in place to report information, such as risks, to the board?

Even without a mandate to do so, is the board searching or planning for future directors who have cyber security expertise?

If so, is the cyber security expertise appropriate, that is to say, does the director possess cyber security expertise, or just a general technology expertise (which does not equate to cyber security expertise)?

What is the plan, i.e., training, to provide all board members with more cyber security knowledge?

Board committee structure

Based on the answers to the questions in the previous board section of the appendix, are conversations warranted for exploring options to the current board structure for cyber security oversight?

What is the timeframe for any changes that may be needed?

What is the new board committee strategy for topic depth, frequency, and attendees?

Does the new governance/oversight model include deep dives into the specifics of the cyber security program outside of the committee meetings?

(Continued)

Section Two		
Security operations	Detection	How complete is the deployment and coverage of endpoint sensors on your systems; where/why are their gaps?
		Are the endpoint protection sensors capable of being turned off by the end user, or are they locked in such a way to prevent uninstall and reconfiguration?
		Does the protection work offline, when the computer or system is not connected to the corporate network?
		Whether insourced or outsourced, does the monitoring provide 24x7x365 coverage with zero gaps in time?
	SIEM	Does the company have adequate logging of systems to provide important machine and user data?
		Does the company use a platform to correlate all of the logs and machine data? Is the coverage adequate to include logs from all systems: security, IT, cloud, etc.?
		Is the pricing model for the SIEM platform optimal to provide the most value (not necessarily inexpensive)?
	Vulnerability management	Does the vulnerability management program include scanning all systems for vulnerabilities? If not, why are there gaps (i.e., licensing, other)?
		Are the metrics for patching performance done by information security or audit, rather than IT who most likely performs the patching?
		Is there an emergency patching process for critical patches that require immediate attention?
		What are the SLOs for patching all severities of vulnerabilities? Are those SLOs reasonable to protect the business with a balance of business needs?

Application security	Does the company follow a SDLC process that produces a phased, secure process for application development of all types?
	Are there training opportunities directed to software developers in your company about the risks, vulnerabilities, threats, and impact of security on coding practices?
	Does the company perform application testing prior to release?
	Does the testing program include both static and dynamic testing?
	Are there impacts to software delivery because of security testing; if so, what is the plan for increasing speed to market for applications?
Artificial intelligence	Has there been analysis for the demand of AI and generative AI use in your business?
	Has a policy for AI use been implemented in your company to prevent the unauthorized usage of sensitive data types?
	Does the security program for AI focus on the technology, or the behaviors that need to be controlled (maintaining confidentiality, integrity, and availability of data)?
	Is the data that emerges from AI technologies checked for accuracy prior to making decisions based off of the data?
Cloud security	Is there an accurate inventory of all enterprise cloud providers for your company, i.e., AWS, Microsoft, Google, etc.?
	Are the roles between the service provider and your company clear in the areas of securing the cloud infrastructure(s)?

(Continued)

		Does your cloud infrastructure employ a zero-trust model?
		What is the level of cloud monitoring for security, performance, billing, usage, etc.?
		Are there strong identity and access management controls in place for your cloud environments? Users and system-to-system access.
		Does your cloud security program include platforms the provide workload protection, identification of risks such as misconfiguration, etc.?
	Identity and access management	Does your company follow a least privileged model of providing just enough access for an authorized person to perform their role and nothing more?
		Are the identity and access profiles reviewed regularly to ensure that access needs have not changed?
		Does your company leverage multifactor authentication? What types of MFA are used, i.e., SMS, code generation, authentication application, etc.?
		How does the company reduce the threat of MFA fatigue and unauthorized authentications?
		Is the MFA deployment strategy incremental in nature through testing, or is it trying to deploy MFA all at once?
Incident response	Incident reporting	How are incidents communicated to the board? Does it include all incidents, or only those that are material?
		How are incidents communicated to third parties, specifically external audit and outside counsel? Is there a good definition between the parties on what a material cyber security incident is?

Incident updates	Is there a formalized process for material incidents being reported to the board? Thresholds for what is material? Who is contacted on the board of material incidents and by whom from the management team?
	During an incident, is there a process for the frequency of incident updates that allows for the free flow of information, balanced by providing time for the responders to provide incident response?
	Are the updates focused on remediation of issues, or do they sometimes stray to educational awareness that could be done in other forums?
Response type	Is the response focused on the type of attack, i.e., website defacement and denial of service attacks, vs. nation-state attacks done under stealth?
External support	Does your company leverage a *paid* incident response retainer with a company that has strong cyber security response expertise?
	Does your incident response provider utilize the endpoint sensors already deployed on your network, or would they require time to deploy their own sensors?
	Is your incident response provider on the list of preferred and/or approved providers by your outside counsel and cyber insurance providers?
Privileged responses	Is there a threshold for what responses are considered to be standard and which will be under privilege?
	If under privilege, is there a process/agreement to ensure the CISO is updated with information pertaining to the response?

(*Continued*)

Incident response plan	Does the company have a well-documented incident response policy and plan? Is it well understood by all stakeholders?
	Is the response plan updated regularly?
	Has the response plan been reviewed by an external cyber security firm to ensure completeness?
	Is the plan made up of all core elements such as reporting, roles/responsibilities, communication plan, and incident handling procedures?
	Does the incident response plan include external stakeholders such as outside counsel, external PR firms, etc.?
	Is there an "out of band" communication method in case the internal communication channels (corporate email) are compromised or out of service?
Response activities	Does the plan include resource allocation, sending some employees home at the start to ensure there is a fresh team of responders after the first team has worked for many hours?
	Is there a mechanism for tracking the time all responders (internal and external) working on the response so that costs associated with the incident can be calculated?
	Is there a pre-developed process for communications to employees, external partners, and customers? Are there appropriate resources available for the many requests for information by partners?
Ransomware response	Is there a pre-determined process for deciding if a ransom will be paid or not paid?

		Who is the executive responsible for making the decision to pay or not to pay? Who is the backup executive in case the primary is unavailable?
		Has the company identified a third-party negotiator to facilitate discussions between the company and the adversary?
	Turning policy into practice	Does the company perform table-top exercises that simulate a cyber event to practice the response steps?
		Are the appropriate stakeholders (internal and external) included in the exercise?
		What is the frequency of the table-top exercises?
		Is the exercise facilitated by a third party with expertise in responding to cyber breaches?
		Does the exercise include scenarios that consider your business, types of attacks, and adversaries who target your industry?
		Are there "injects" in the exercise designed to disrupt the flow of the response, i.e., stock price drops, journalist requesting comment, etc.?
Security awareness	Annual training	Does the company perform annual training on security for all employees? Is completion of the training tracked to each employee?
	Awareness articles	Does your security team deliver regular cyber security awareness articles to the employees?
		Are the articles timely insofar as topics relate to the threat trends currently being seen by the security operations team, or perhaps online purchasing safety during the holiday season?

(Continued)

	Is there a calendar of topics to be delivered each month to ensure duplicate subject matter is not consistently delivered? Does the calendar allow for shifts in subject matter based on threats being seen by the security operations team at the company?
	Is there a process for emergency types of articles?
Role-based training	Does the security awareness program conduct job specific security training that focus on the risks associated with more sensitive types of roles, i.e., system administrator, executive, administrative assistant, etc.?
Brown bag sessions	Are there voluntary types of security training opportunities for employees to learn more about cyber security?
Cyber security awareness month	Does the security program offer innovative awareness activities during the month of October – Cyber security awareness month?
Awareness options	Does the security team provide unique awareness opportunities such as giveaways, security open house, etc. to help employees retain critical cyber security knowledge?
Internal phishing campaigns	Is security training made personal for the employee through internal phishing campaigns delivered by the security team?
	Do these campaigns measure the effectiveness across the enterprise, teams, and individual levels?
	Is there a process for additional training for those employees who fail multiple campaigns?
	Do the campaigns start with easy to identify phishing emails and move to more complex ones that are difficult to spot?

Policy management	Policy structure	Does the company have a robust cyber security policy program in place?
		Are the documents separated by policy, procedure, standards, guidelines, etc., or are they all combined in one long hard to read document?
		Are the policies written (as much as possible) in language that is easy for employees who may not have technical knowledge to understand?
		Are policies brief, succinct, and reference more detailed documentation such as procedures, standards, and guidelines?
		Are the policies easy to access by all employees?
		Is the policy management program automated to reduce multiple versions of documents being sent back and forth via email?
		Is there a waiver process in place that allows for temporary relief from mandates to allow users/teams to come into compliance?
Risk management	Enterprise risk management	Is the CISO an active participant in the ERM program or do they merely update cyber security risks and deliver them to a larger team where someone else presents and the team discusses?
	Risk management process	Does the risk management process include the creation and ongoing maintenance of a risk register to log applicable risks to the enterprise?
		Is the risk register reviewed and updated regularly?
	Third-party risk	Does the company have a robust program for assessing the risk of third-party partners and vendors?

(Continued)

	Is there a good process for inventorying all vendors associated with your business? When new vendors are onboarded, is there a policy to mandate that they go through a risk management evaluation?
Assessment process	Is the third-party risk assessment process automated or does it rely on emailing questionnaires back and forth between the vendor and your company?
	Are the questionnaires designed for different types of partnerships: direct access to your corporate network, little access to sensitive data/ network, no access to sensitive data/ network?
	Are there regular reviews of the vendor relationship to ensure the scope of services provided have not changed from the original assessment?

Index

Note: Endnotes are indicated by the page number followed by "n" and the note number e.g., 11n1 refers to note 1 on page 11. Page numbers in **bold** refers to Tables.

Printed in the United States
by Baker & Taylor Publisher Services